CREEPING COMPROMISE

BY JOE CREWS

Published by:

Homeward Publishing

P.O. Box 357
Yorba Linda, CA 92885
Copyright © 2002
All Rights Reserved

Memorial Edition with Indexes - 4th printing 2011
Memorial Edition with Indexes - 3rd printing 2008
Memorial Edition with Indexes - 2nd printing 2003
Memorial Edition with Indexes - 1st Printing 2002

Cover by Cherry Dezign
Typesetting by Robert Bethel
Layout by Elizabeth Barnes

To order: 1-800-823-0481

ISBN #0-938805-04-5

Printed in the United States of America
by Barnes Printing

Crews' Contemporaries' Comment

Doug Batchelor, President, Speaker, Amazing Facts: "With his unique, straight-forward style, Brother Crews addresses some of the most sensitive and controversial issues in a bold uncompromising approach. This classic work made its mark 25 years ago and has been stirring Laodicean Christians ever since."

Elder E. E. Cleveland, Lecturer in the Dept. of Religion at Oakwood College: "The works of Elder Joe Crews recommend themselves by their Biblical orthodoxy and the clarity with which the author speaks and writes. While I hesitate to endorse every method of expression, I nevertheless believe in his Biblical conclusions and heartily recommend his written works."

Alvin M. Kibble, Vice-President, North American Division of Seventh-day Adventists: "A bold visionary leader, Pastor Joe Crews took his calling and ministry seriously. Committed unwaveringly to firm traditional values, he preached and taught a strong doctrine and believed what he preached. He endeavored to hold up the principles of "his faith." Not always enthusiastic of his fellow leaders, Pastor Crews raised a less than casual objection to decisions and actions he felt had a compromising effect upon the mission and mandates of the Church. Always endeavoring to work within the organization of his church, his ministry effected a balance among the ministry of his contemporaries, by raising the conscience of the faith community on matters of Christian standard and practice."

Pat Langley, Prayer Coordinator, North eastern Conference of Seventh-day Adventists, Family Life Education: "I would unhesitatingly recommend the book, *Creeping Compromise.* Reading this book has changed my life, it will yours, too."

Jan Paulsen, President, General Conference of Seventh-day Adventists: "Reflection on the ministry and witness of Elder Joe Crews and Amazing Facts reveals a man who understood he was commissioned by God to share the blessed hope found in Jesus with the members of the church as well as the 'stranger.' From the spoken word, and from the books and magazines, which Elder Crews authored and published, many individuals have come to know Jesus more personally. The ministry of this man has been a blessing to many."

Don C. Schneider, President, North American Division: "We have a hard time reaching the cities today. We did 40 years ago too, but Elder Joe Crews took the challenge of Elder Cyril Miller and Elder Bill May to start a ministry that would reach Baltimore. The Amazing Facts Ministry that Joe Crews started in response to that challenge has reached far more than Baltimore—and the church is grateful to him."

Benjamin D. Schoun, President, Atlantic Union Conference of Seventh-day Adventists, former Associate Dean of the Theological Seminary, Andrews University: "For Christian believers who have received the grace of Christ and have the assurance of salvation, this book points out life-style practices that can safeguard and strengthen one's devotion and submissions to Christ. While Christians may conscientiously draw lines of practice in somewhat different places, the principles articulated here are worthy to consider and follow."

G. Ralph Thompson, retired Secretary of the General Conference of Seventh-day Adventists: "For many years it was my privilege to listen to Joe Crews on his radio program called 'Amazing Facts.' His dynamic style of delivery and his fearless presentation of the Everlasting Gospel made a tremendous impression upon thousands of listeners and many of them were led to accept the Advent Message.

"His broadcast was on some of the radio programs in the Caribbean where I happened to be the Conference and later, a Union President, and we were blessed by his ministry. I also was on Radio Barbados as speaker for the 'Faith for Today' weekly radio broadcast every Sunday for 25 years and to have our people being also able to listen to 'Amazing Facts' from Montserrat and elsewhere at other times, was a great blessing. We were kindred spirits, engaged in the same type of outreach and soul winning, proclaiming the good news of the Advent Message.

"Something even more uncanny happened to both of us years later. In 1990, I had to enter Washington Adventist Hospital to undergo an angioplasty to correct a heart problem.

"Joe Crews entered the same hospital with the same type of problem. The operation was successful, and he was looking forward to going home to resume his broadcasting when he suddenly had a relapse and to the shock of family and friends, never made it back.

"As a fellow broadcaster, I felt keenly his loss, but his work and sacrifice live on as an inspiration to countless others.

"Joe Crews was indeed a BRAVE WARRIOR FOR CHRIST. May his tribe increase!!"

PREFACE

It was a hot summer day under a large canvas tent at a camp-meeting in the State of Maryland. We were newly baptized Christians who, on that day, found ourselves seated on the platform under that tent where we had been invited to give our testimony and special music. Seated beside us on the rostrum was the principle speaker for the camp-meeting. And, speak he did!

In a tactful and gracious way, he presented cutting truths entreating the listener to come up to a higher Christian standard, mentally, physically and spiritually. He spoke as one sincerely concerned about the eternal salvation of each one within his hearing. This was our first introduction to Joe Crews.

There are so few strong men today who not only see the evils and abominations of the time but can present them fearlessly, tactfully and lovingly to God's people. As the opportunity was given to us to publish our own book, *Thy Nakedness, Lord What Shall I Wear?*, we wanted someone to review it and write their comments for the back cover. Joe Crews graciously accepted.

Over the years he has been an inspiration and encouragement to our ministry. He pastored, taught and personally evangelized by television, radio, the writing of books and the *Amazing Facts Study Guides* (1-14), always giving very pertinent information to the last days in which we live. The various facets of his ministry have been instrumental in introducing thousands to Jesus Christ.

By no stretch of imagination, while sitting under that camp-meeting tent, could we have ever dreamed that years later we would be afforded the privilege of having a small part in continuing the Joe Crews legacy by being the publishers of one of his first and most important books, *Creeping Compromise*.

The principles and good "common sense" presented in *Creeping Compromise* have strengthened and encouraged us to stay on track as we have read and re-read the godly counsel on its pages. We pray that you, the reader, will have the same experience.

Homeward Publishing
Rick and Gwen Shorter, Directors

Table of Contents

INTRODUCTION 5

OUR ENEMY—THE WORLD 8

IS NUDITY MODEST? 21

DOUBLE STANDARD EXPOSED 30

UNISEX 38

COLORFUL COSMETICS AND JEWELRY 45

TELEVISION TRAP 70

LAWFULLY JOINED 79

MUSIC AND MOODS 86

MEAT OR UNMEAT 92

POTLUCKS AND PRINCIPLES 99

DESTROYING YOUR WITNESS 105

LEGALISM OR LOVE.. 113

INDEX.. 117

SPIRIT OF PROPHECY INDEX 124

Whether therefore ye eat, or drink, or whatsoever ye do, do all to the glory of God.
1 Corinthians 10:31

Behold, I come quickly: hold that fast which thou hast, that no man take thy crown.
Revelation 3:11

INTRODUCTION

The subject of Christian standards is probably one of the most neglected doctrines in the modern church. Very little is in print today that can provide even elementary instruction in this vital area. Only a few small books or tracts have attempted to deal with the basic and practical principles which should distinguish the Christian life from that of the world.

The reason for this reluctance to write on these specifics of Christian conduct probably rests upon two fears: First, the fear of offending the rather large majority of church members who are living far below the biblical standard. Second, the fear of being labeled as judgmental, legalistic, holier-than-thou, and lacking in the personal, love-relationship with Christ.

We are forced to recognize that these fears have often been justified. There has been too much written in the spirit of pharisaism. Satan has exploited the vocal, fanatical views of a very few and has used them to intimidate those who would write temperately on the subject. And too often, in his special hatred of this truth, Satan has caused many in the church to look upon any discussion of Christian standards as extremist and improper.

These factors have combined to create a dearth of material on this subject. For this reason, if for no other, a tremendous need exists for educating the church on balanced biblical principles of conduct—principles that conflict in no way with the concepts of righteousness by faith which should underlie the lifestyle of every true Christian.

We also must concede that little should need to be said on this subject. After all, the actions are not the means of gaining salvation. We are saved by grace through faith and not by merit of works, obedience, or outward conduct on our part. Any overemphasis on these external things could be easily misinterpreted as a denial of justification by faith.

Obviously, at the time of this writing no such overemphasis exists on a denominational level. Only occasional lone voices are heard on this subject. On the other hand, there is a spectacular resurgence of preaching on the doctrine of righteousness by faith, which is the way it should be. When preached in its true setting the greatest need of the church today is to know more about the experiential relationship of justification and sanctification. But in presenting those deep spiritual truths of salvation nothing should be said to downgrade the importance of obedience. Some seem almost incapable of maintaining the beautiful balance between faith and works. *But this is so important and necessary!* To misunderstand either grace or works is to stultify the experience and thwart the personal witness.

Some may object that a book like this is not needed, because the outward conduct is a natural, spontaneous outgrowth of conversion to Christ. Therefore, the life will automatically produce the fruit of true obedience and righteousness. But is this totally true? It is true that the actions spring from the internal attitude of conversion, but instruction is needed for the most committed Christian.

Many converted people keep Sunday and smoke cigarettes simply because no one has explained to them the biblical objections to those actions. Are we being legalistic in teaching them to change their conduct on the basis of the Word of God? Then could it be wrong to talk about other areas of outward conduct which might need harmonizing with the Bible?

One final observation should be made before you begin reading the pages which follow. The doctrine of Christian standards is for spiritual people only. This book is not written for the unconverted. Indeed, it will appear only as a lot of foolishness to the worldly class.

Please do not take the things which are presented in this book and seek to impose them upon your unregenerate family or friends. Especially are we counseled against forcing dress standards on those who are not converted. Listen to this warning:

"You cannot possibly change the heart. To get up a different style of dress will not do it. The difficulty is, the church needs converting daily....Those who venture to disobey the plainest statements of inspiration will not heed any human efforts made to induce them to wear a plain, neat, unadorned, proper dress....To those who are making self their idol, nothing in the line of human tests should be presented, for it would only give them an excuse for making the final plunge into apostasy." *Our Health Message,* pp. 429-430.

Apply the principles of this book to your own life. Some of them have seldom been seen in print before. Restrain the impulse to call them fanatical until you have read the entire book and have asked God to show you what to do about them in the fading light of earth's last sunset.

OUR ENEMY—THE WORLD

The world today is in an incredible state of flux and change. Traditional views and values have been altered and almost reversed within a relatively short time. Under the numbing influence of television and the highly mobile electronic media, minds have been manipulated, thought patterns set up, and decisions dictated. And most of the millions so influenced are almost oblivious to the powerful artificial agencies which were used to change their minds and their morals.

There is no question whatsoever that Satan is pulling the strings and directing the subtle forces which are designed to destroy us spiritually. Under the hypnotizing influence of these forces, Christian minds have been just as successfully brainwashed as those of the most unregenerate sinner.

Our only safety is to recognize the clever camouflages of the enemy. A thousand disguised death traps have been planted all around us. Almost imperceptibly our thinking has been affected by what we see and hear. Spiritual convictions have softened and disappeared altogether. The fine sensitivity to sin has been blunted by incessant exposure to the apparent innocent influences of our baited society.

In the Scriptures these assault weapons of Satan are referred to simply as "the world." And no one can say that we have not been warned against their demoralizing effect. Paul, James, and John all wrote with dramatic urgency about the dangers of collaborating with the world:

"Love not the world, neither the things that are in the world. If any man love the world, the love of the Father is not in him. For all that is in the world, the lust of the flesh, and the lust of the eyes, and the pride of life, is not of the Father, but is of the world." 1 John 2:15, 16.

"Ye adulterers and adulteresses, know ye not that the friendship of the world is enmity with God? Whosoever therefore will be a friend of the world is the enemy of God." James 4:4.

"If ye were of the world, the world would love his own: but because ye are not of the world, but I have chosen you out of the world, therefore the world hateth you." John 15:19.

"Wherefore come out from among them, and be ye separate, saith the Lord, and touch not the unclean thing; and I will receive you." 2 Corinthians 6:17.

"Who gave himself for us, that he might redeem us from all iniquity, and purify unto himself a peculiar people, zealous of good works." Titus 2:14.

These writers had an inspired obsession to expose the deadly error of mingling together the sacred and profane. They are saying to us with one voice, "Don't love the world. You are not of the world. Come out of the world and be a peculiar and separated people."

These texts are not to be construed as orders to leave the physical occupation of the world. Obviously, they are warnings against certain influences, customs, and ideas which would be highly detrimental to the Christian way of life. Furthermore, Jesus Himself indicated that things of the world would appear completely innocent in the eyes of men. He laid down an eternal principle when He spoke these words to the Pharisees: "For that which is highly esteemed among men is abomination in the sight of God." Luke 16:15.

Study that statement carefully. Christ is saying that the most honored, respected things in society will be the greatest enemy of the truth. He is saying that His people would have to stand on the opposite side from the prevailing practices of the world. True Christians will have to reject the lifestyle which will be the accepted, approved norm for all the rest of the world. Do we have any idea what is involved in taking such a position? It is not easy to stand against the sincere, articulate opinions of popular national figures. And then there will be full support from the great church systems to give even more credence to the things which are "highly esteemed among men." This wrong way of life will be so patently taken for granted that any deviation will be looked upon as stupid and irrational. E. G. White explains it thus: "When we reach the standard that the Lord would have us reach, worldlings will regard Seventh-day Adventists as odd, singular, strait-laced extremists." *Fundamentals of Christian Education*, p. 289.

This brings us to another most important question: What effect will all of these glamorized, disguised approaches have upon the remnant church? The studied purpose of our great enemy is to make sin appear unobjectionable, and if possible, to infiltrate the camp of the saints. The one great citadel of strength, the last bulwark of defense which stands against the lawless one, is the seed of the woman. According to Revelation 12:17, "The dragon was wroth with the woman, and went to make war with the remnant of her seed, which keep the commandments of God, and have the testimony of Jesus Christ."

Satan hates the law of God. He hates the Sabbath. And he hates those who stand in the gap, upholding the validity of that law. Down through the centuries the devil has devised special weapons to use against the people of God. Those weapons have varied from generation to generation. Often the sharp edge of persecution was turned against the little remnant who stood loyal to the commandments of God.

Persecution and the death sentence will come into the picture again as a desperate devil unleashes the worst that he has against the true church. He knows this is the life or death encounter which will settle the issues of the great controversy for all eternity. This time he will overlook no advantage. Relying upon the psychological expertise of 6,000 years' experience of trying to bend the human mind, he has initiated a softening-up operational plan against the people he hates. That plan consists of gradually weakening the spiritual defenses of Seventh-day Adventists through worldly compromise. This will be the ultimate weapon which Satan has cleverly designed to undermine the faith of every member of the remnant church.

How successful will it be? How many will be shaken out in the approaching crisis because they yielded to the things of the world? We don't have to wonder. The answer has been given over and over in the Spirit of Prophecy. It is a sickening answer, and we would like to believe it is not true. But read it and marvel:

"I would say that we are living in a most solemn time. In the last vision given me, I was shown the startling fact that but a small portion of those who now profess the truth will be sanctified by it and be saved. Many will get above the simplicity of the work. They will conform to the world, cherish idols, and become spiritually dead." *Testimonies for the Church*, Vol. 1, pp. 608-609.

How incredible! The great majority of those who now rejoice in the truth will give up their faith and be lost. They will be lost because they "conform to the world." Satan's insidious, innocent appearing, highly esteemed lifestyle will disarm them, weaken them, and finally destroy them. Another statement is even more specific: "The great proportion of those who now appear genuine will prove to be base metal." *Testimonies for the Church*, Vol. 5, p. 136.

The softening-up strategy of the enemy is clearly described by E. G. White in these words: "The time is not far distant when the test will come to every soul. The observance of the false sabbath will be urged upon us. The contest will be between the commandments of God and the commandments of men. Those who have yielded step by step to worldly demands, and conformed to worldly customs, will then yield to the powers that be, rather than subject themselves to derision, insult, threatened imprisonment, and death. At that time the gold will be separated from the dross. True godliness will be clearly distinguished from the appearance and tinsel of it. Many a star that we have admired for its brilliance will then go out in darkness. Those who have assumed the ornaments of the sanctuary, but are not clothed with Christ's righteousness, will then appear in the shame of their own nakedness." *Prophets and Kings*, p. 188.

Don't miss the line which describes the reason for this mass apostasy. "Those who have yielded step by step to worldly demands, and conformed to worldly customs, will then yield to the powers that be."

Not only will the majority be shaken out of the church, they will actually turn against their former brethren and become bitter enemies of the truth.

"As the storm approaches, a large class who have professed faith in the third angel's message, but have not been sanctified through obedience to the truth, abandon their position and join the ranks of the opposition. By uniting with the world and partaking of its spirit, they have come to view matters in nearly the same light; and when the test is brought, they are prepared to choose the easy, popular side. Men of talent and pleasing address, who once rejoiced in the truth, employ their powers to deceive and mislead souls. They become the most bitter enemies of their former brethren. When Sabbath keepers are brought before the courts to answer for their faith, these apostates are the most efficient agents for Satan to misrepresent and accuse them, and by false reports and insinuations to stir up the rulers against them." *The Great Controversy*, p. 608.

Again we are fascinated by the expression, "By uniting with the world...they are prepared to choose the easy, popular side." Notice that it is a preparation work— "They are prepared...." Here again is revealed the fantastic psychological program of Satan to break down moral barriers. Worldly compromise. Worldly conformity. "The work which the church has failed to do in a time of peace and prosperity, she will have to do in a terrible crisis, under most discouraging, forbidding circumstances. The warnings that worldly conformity has silenced or withheld, must be given under the fiercest opposition from enemies of the faith. And at that time the superficial, conservative class, whose influence has steadily retarded the progress of the work, will renounce the faith, and take their stand with its avowed enemies, toward whom their sympathies have long been tending. These apostates will then manifest the most bitter enmity, doing all in their power to oppress and malign their former brethren and to excite indignation against them. This day is just before us." *Testimonies for the Church*, Vol. 1, p. 278.

The words "worldly conformity" spring out at us again from this statement. Repeatedly we have been warned about this massive attack of Satan through worldliness. Yet, we hear so very little about this particular subject. Thousands of Seventh-day Adventists have been blinded to this operational plan of the evil one. Some of our people have been led to believe that it is legalistic to make any kind of issue over standards and lifestyles. To them it is "quibbling" and judgmental. This is surely the way Satan would have them feel. They talk and think much about the final test over the true Sabbath, but fail to see how *the outcome of the test is being determined right now*.

Says Ellen White: "Those who are uniting with the world are receiving the worldly mold and preparing for the mark of the beast. Those who are distrustful of self, who are humbling themselves before God, and purifying their souls by obeying the truth—these are receiving the heavenly mold and preparing for the seal of God in their foreheads." *Testimonies for the Church*, Vol. 5, p. 216.

The mark of the beast will be enforced. Every soul will have to go to the side of the true Sabbath or the counterfeit, Sunday. Seventh-day Adventists will face the death sentence for their faith. And, tragically, the majority will not be able to stand in the crisis. They will prove disloyal because of earlier compromise and vacillation over Christian standards. By yielding gradually to worldly custom and fashion their strength of will and decision will be so diluted that they can not endure the test. And this compromise is going on right now! This very moment the great majority of our fellow church members are bending toward the world to such a degree that they will be lost when the mark is enforced.

Here's the question that bothers me: Am I bending with them? How can I be sure that I'm not following the drift which will bring on the great shaking in the church? What cleverly disguised, diabolical method has Satan employed to blind the eyes of so many of God's people that they will finally choose the world over the truth? It must surely be the polished masterpiece of all the deceptive plans he has ever used against the saints. The people who have been noted for their high standards will be tricked into yielding up their separated lifestyle. The average Adventist today would indignantly deny that he is being worldly. The majority of our members would express full assurance that they will not give up their faith, even in the face of death. *Yet we have just read that they will!*

What does this mean? It means that most of our members are caught up in worldliness and don't even realize it. They are indulging in dangerous compromise and think it is perfectly innocent and acceptable. They have been so blinded that they can not recognize the worldly things they are doing.

Why can they not see their involvement with the world? Because the lowering of standards was so gradual that none realized what was happening. The devil's scheme is not to make the church suddenly abandon its historic position against the flesh and the world. He is far too clever to think we will make any public announcement that it's all right to go to movies, wear makeup and jewelry, or drink tea and coffee.

But Satan knows how the mind operates under the power of suggestion and association. With infinite patience he introduces pictures, words, ideas, and practices that can not be condemned per se. In fact, many of Satan's "innocent" devices are not only highly esteemed among men, but have some commendable qualities and features. A perfect example of such a device is television. And how many of us have heard convincing arguments for the fine news, documentaries, and religious programming. No one can say that the TV console in the living room is an evil thing in itself. Taken by itself it is a fine piece of furniture and a source of good information.

Then begins the masterful process of psychological assault in which Satan is unexcelled. Very slowly the discriminations are dulled by glimpses and snatches of borderline comedy, violence, etc. The mind adjusts to the new level of input, and almost imperceptibly begins to tolerate the changing quality of sight and sound.

Two inspired statements will help us see how the work of the enemy develops:

"Satan will insinuate himself by little wedges, which widen as they make a place for themselves. The specious devices of Satan will be brought into the special work of God at this time." *Selected Messages*, Book 2, p. 21.

"The work of the enemy is not abrupt....It is a secret undermining of the strongholds of principle. It begins in apparently small things." *Patriarchs and Prophets*, p. 718.

How important it is to recognize the direction in which we are being led by any particular influence. The manner in which quail are often trapped provides a parallel to Satan's tactics. Wheat is placed several feet from the spot where a snare is triggered to spring shut on the quail. At first the birds approach the good wheat with some obvious apprehension, but because there is no danger in view their fears are allayed.

The next day the wheat is placed a bit nearer to the snare, and the birds are less wary of the scattered grain. Day after day, the wheat is placed just a little bit closer to the trap, until the quail are completely confident that there is nothing dangerous about the fine wheat. Then, of course, the grain is placed inside the snare, and the birds still come. Innocently they trust the good food to remain good, and a safe feast to remain safe. Then the trap is sprung.

I'm not contending that quails should stop eating wheat or that Christians should cease all good activities. The point is that we should be cautious enough to consider the direction in which we are being led and be willing to give up even the "good" things if they are taking us in a direction of spiritual danger.

Can good things lead in the wrong direction? Indeed they can. Christians are led to give up their high standards by degrees, often by a completely innocent-looking process.

This is the way compromise has always slipped into the church. Satan introduces an activity which is only slightly objectionable. In fact, it might be very hard to define exactly why the action isn't good. And because the deviation is so tiny no one really wants to make an issue over it. Some faithful members of the church feel uncomfortable about the matter but are reluctant to say anything for fear of being called fanatical. They decide to wait until there is a larger issue before they take a strong stand.

Unfortunately, there will never be a larger issue. The devil makes certain that all the steps of compromise are very small. He knows that hardly anyone would have the courage to make any sustained objection to the minute degree of digression.

Once upon a time, the devil's favorite argument was, "Everybody else is doing it." Although the young people still use that one occasionally, a new term is currently being tossed about to justify worldly conformity: "A little bit is all right." The dress is just a little bit too short. The drink contains only a little bit of caffeine. The TV program shows only a little bit of violence. The wedding ring is only a small one, and the cosmetics add just a little bit of color. We could go on and on.

We can't seem to learn the lesson of Lot as he left Sodom. Most of his family had refused to leave the doomed city. He had lost everything he owned by choosing to live in that wicked environment—his home, wealth, and lovely daughters. But when the angels urged him to flee into the mountains, he begged for permission to move into another city! And his rationalization was, "Is it not a little one?" Genesis 19:20.

How could he do that? Surely Lot had learned that the cities had almost destroyed him. Since the day he "pitched his tent toward Sodom" the family had inched almost imperceptibly toward involvement with the corrupt society of the inner city. Little by little the transition was made from borderline neutrality to tongue-in-cheek participation.

When Lot pleaded to live in yet another city, he was demonstrating dramatically how gradual compromise can blind the senses and distort the judgment.

How many in the modern church have long ago pitched their tent toward Sodom? How many have taken that first, easily justified step toward compromise? And how many fellow Christians felt uneasy about it but had not the courage to raise a warning? Later, what happened? Those desensitized Christians began to defend the progressive drift of lowering standards by the same argument, "Is it not a little one?" Does this not explain how worldliness has crept even into the remnant church? For example: How did the miniskirt abomination become such a familiar sight in Seventh-day Adventist churches on Sabbath morning? Sister White explains how it happened with the hoop skirts in another generation, and you can see how Satan used the same subtlety to introduce the miniskirt.

"The power of example is great. Sister A ventures to wear small hoops. Sister B says: It is not worse for me to wear hoops than for Sister A, and she wears them a little larger. Sister C imitates the example of Sister A and B, and wears her hoops a little larger than A and B, but all contend that their hoops are small." *Testimonies for the Church*, Vol. 1, p. 278.

Does that sound familiar? Girls and ladies alike in the remnant church began to inch up in their hemlines. If the knee length was all right, then what was wrong with half an inch above the knee? If it was modest at a half-inch above, then how could another half inch make it immodest?

Why was so little said about it in protest? Because every stage of the leavening process was too small to stir an alarm. Not even the ministry realized what was really taking place. Many dared speak out, but they were quickly silenced by charges of having an evil mind. Very few continued to blow the trumpet of warning against the growing violation of modesty.

How can we explain the blanket of silence that often attends these specious intrusions of the world? Apparently much of it is rooted in the fear of offending.

"I saw that individuals would rise up against the plain testimonies. It does not suit their natural feelings. They would choose to have smooth things spoken unto them, and have peace cried in their ears. I view the church in a more dangerous condition than they ever have been. Experimental religion is known by but a few. The shaking must soon take place to purify the church.

"Preachers should have no scruples to preach the truth as it is found in God's Word. Let the truth out. I have been shown that why ministers have not more success is, they are afraid of hurting feelings, fearful of not being courteous, and they lower the standard of truth and conceal if possible the peculiarity of our faith. I saw that God could not make such successful. The truth must be made pointed, and the necessity of a decision urged. And as false shepherds are crying, Peace, and are preaching smooth things, the servants of God must cry aloud and spare not, and leave the result with God." *Spiritual Gifts*, Vol. II, pp. 284-285.

"By some there is a shunning of the living testimony. Cutting truths must not be shunned. It needs something besides theory to reach hearts now. It needs the stirring testimony to alarm and arouse;

that will stir the enemy's subjects, and then honest souls will be led to decide for the truth. There has been, and still is, with some a disposition to have everything move on very smoothly. They see no necessity of straight testimony.

"Sins exist in the church, that God hates, but they are scarcely touched for fear of making enemies. Opposition has risen in the church to the plain testimony. Some will not bear it. They wish smooth things spoken unto them. And if the wrongs of individuals are touched, they complain of severity, and sympathize with those in the wrong....When the church departs from God they despise the plain testimony, and complain of severity and harshness. It is a sad evidence of the lukewarm state of the church." *Spiritual Gifts*, Vol. II, pp. 283-284.

The great need is for courageous ministers who will speak boldly about right and wrong. The pastor who truly loves his flock and his God will not hesitate to call sin by its right name in every discourse. Straight forward preaching, which creates concern over wrong doing, is the most genuine demonstration of true love. Such men will weep much over their flock and with their flock, but they will not withhold the message which can heal and restore.

Dietrich Bonhoeffer in his book *Life Together* made this significant statement: "Nothing can be more cruel than the tenderness that consigns another to his sin. Nothing can be more compassionate than the severe rebuke that calls a brother back from the path of sin." A paragraph from the book *Patriarchs and Prophets* has influenced my own ministry more than any other thing I have read outside of the Bible. Its solemn message has burned in my soul from the first time I read it soon after ordination. It applies equally to parents as well as to pastors. So, for me it has double impact.

"Those who have too little courage to reprove wrong, or who through indolence or lack of interest make no earnest effort to purify the family or the church of God, are held accountable for the evil that may result from the neglect of duty. We are just as responsible for evils that we might have checked in others by exercise of parental or pastoral authority, as if the acts had been our own." *Patriarchs and Prophets*, p. 578.

Don't miss the thrust of that statement. If I am afraid to blow the trumpet and warn God's people of approaching spiritual danger, and they are led into sin as a consequence, then I will be held as accountable for those sins as if they were my own. I don't want to answer for the sins of others. That's one reason I am writing this book. Too few are hearing about the covert tactics of our great enemy to break down the strength of the church today.

The only way we are going to stop this worldly encroachment is to draw a line somewhere, and stand on it. The nibbling away of our standards will continue until we muster the courage to resist the first compromise. Mrs. White said, "The distance is widening between Christ and His people, and lessening between them and the world." *Spiritual Gifts*, Vol. IV, p. 68. Again she wrote: "Our only safety is to stand as God's peculiar people. We must not yield one inch to the customs and fashions of this degenerate age, but stand in moral independence, making no compromise with its corrupt and idolatrous practices." *Testimonies for the Church*, Vol. 5, p. 78.

It will be our purpose in the following chapters to study certain large areas of Christian standards which Satan has made the special focus of his plan of creeping compromise.

IS NUDITY MODEST?

The dress question has probably been the most sensitive area in which to draw lines based upon biblical principle. Disagreement over definition of terms has frightened many ministers away from the subject. What is modesty and immodesty? Other concerned church spokesmen have been troubled by the angry charge of liberals that dress critics themselves are obsessed with evil minds.

Some have even made a gross misapplication of righteousness by faith and have taken the position that any discussion of external conduct constitutes a legalistic denial of Christ's imputed righteousness.

Does this subject merit a few specific observations? Has it been over emphasized? How many books have rolled from our church presses on the subject? No one can say that it has suffered from over exposure. Hardly a tract or leaflet has expounded on the matter, and few of our books give it any appreciable recognition as a spiritual problem.

But is it spiritual problem? Listen to this statement from *Testimonies for the Church*, Vol. 4, p. 647: "Fashion is deteriorating the intellect and eating out the spirituality of our people. Obedience to fashion is pervading our Seventh-day Adventist churches, and is doing more than any other power to separate our people from God." If this could be said of the dress problem over a hundred years ago, what could be said about it in these days of unisex, the bikini, and toplessness?

Although the miniskirt comes and goes on the fashion scene, there will always be an element of nudity in prevailing styles that needs to be recognized as immodest and unchristian. Lest some should quibble over that word "modesty" let us not try to define it precisely here. But there can be no debate over the fact that anything which hurts a fellow Christian is wrong. And certainly any kind of dress which causes our fellow man to commit sin must be classified as wrong.

Then let us be honest enough to admit that the exposed human body is quite capable of stirring up sin in both thought and action. Too many have acted very naively toward this mushrooming problem of nudity. It is time to speak very plainly so that both men and women understand the true nature of this evil.

Ann Landers printed this letter in her column at the height of the miniskirt craze several years ago:

"Dear Ann Landers:

"Here's a message from a dirty old man—age 22. I'm a college senior and the point of view I express here reflects the thinking of a lot of guys. There is nothing so ludicrous as a chick in a thighhigh mini, sitting on a chair or sofa, tugging at her skirt, trying to pull it down to cover her status of respectability. She blushes ten shades of red and asks with eyes big as saucers, 'Am I sitting all right?' Or, 'Is anything showing?'

"If they don't want anything to show, why don't they buy a skirt with some material in it? More than once I've gotten a dirty look because I was caught popping an eyeball.

"Please tell the Great Pretenders who feign insult to come off it. The reason why they go half naked is because they want to create a little unrest. Tell them that act should have been cancelled when they accepted the hike of the hem and said 'to Blank' with decency."

Many women have brushed aside criticism of their short dresses by blaming everything on the dirty old men with their evil thoughts. But is that the basic fault? Some months ago I received a telephone call while holding an evangelistic series in the state of Texas. A barber who listened to my daily radio program wanted a personal interview in my motel room. Being a Catholic he did not feel free to attend the public service, but he indicated on the phone that he desperately needed some spiritual counsel.

This man turned out to be a wonderful Christian gentleman. He spoke of his great desire to be saved and to live a godly life. Then he confided the problem. Mini-skirted women came into his barber shop day by day. He prayed and struggled to keep his thoughts pure. With tears in his eyes he asked me, "Is God going to destroy me because I cannot always keep my thoughts clean and holy? Please tell me what to do. I want to be saved and I want to keep my mind upon God, but how can I do it with these half-dressed women before my eyes?"

I felt sorry for that barber. He was wrestling with the same problem that every Christian man and boy has to face. It is not confined to "dirty old men." Every man, woman, and child in the world has a carnal nature by birth. But the male struggle to keep the thoughts straight is based upon more than the fleshly nature. It is rooted in the fact that God created men with a completely different sexual makeup than women.

God made man in the beginning with a very sensitive sexual nature that could be quickly aroused by the *sight* of female nudity. Woman, on the other hand, was created with a sexual nature which would not be so easily stirred, especially by sight. She was made to be more responsive to touch and tenderness. Her more subtle sexuality could be drawn out by the physical attentions involved in the conjugal relationship.

God gave man his emotional sex nature for the purpose of making marriage more pleasurable and happy. The husband was to be the aggressive one in the relationship. Under this beautiful plan of God, the sex instinct of both husband and wife could be lawfully stirred. But mark this: God never intended for man's sex emotions to be stimulated outside the marriage chamber. And in order to protect him God placed within the woman a delicate sense of modest reserve, so that she would not expose her body except to her own husband.

The plan was perfect, but it has broken down in one area. Satan has managed to destroy to a very great extent that inherent modesty with which the Creator endowed womanhood. Under the growing curse of transgression, women have thrown off the moral restraints. Uninhibited nudity or provocative half-dress has become the accepted norm of modem fashion. On every side, the Christian, as well as the non-Christian, is forced to look upon scenes of nakedness which are utterly foreign to the original plan of the Creator.

What has been the effect of this perverted order of things? It has produced a sex-saturated society whose moral qualities just about match those of the antediluvians. Jesus said, "But as the days of Noe were, so shall also the coming of the Son of man be." Matthew 24:37. And what were the conditions of Noah's day which would be duplicated in the end of time? Genesis 6:5 says that "every imagination of the thoughts of his heart was only evil continually."

We have only to look at the sorry state of today's entertainment and communication media to know how fully this prophecy has been fulfilled. Pornography has been legitimized. The TV channels are crowded with lewd sex, either implicit or explicit. The world of advertising, and even the daily news commentaries, are sprinkled with profanity and suggestive double-talk. The imagination of modem man seems obsessed with the subject of sex, often deviant and perverted. Homosexuality has not only received the tolerant coexistence which it sought after, but has been given recognition by the majority of psychiatrists as normal sex behavior.

And what about the Christians who are surrounded by this glorification of the flesh? Unfortunately, it has not been left outside the church doors. Slowly the world edged into the remnant church. By degrees the sight of knees and thighs even in the sanctuary began to be tolerated. The sense of outrage disappeared as we got used to the weekly display.

What about the Christian men whose inherent sex nature is so easily influenced by this nudity? Do they respond to the external stimuli by thinking evil thoughts and committing mental adultery? By the grace of God true Christians can lay hold of victory, even over the imaginations of the heart. Through submission and prayer any man can claim the power of a pure mind, but the styles of dress make it a more difficult struggle.

Jesus made it clear that men are easily led into wrong thinking. He said, "Ye have heard that it was said by them of old time, Thou shalt not commit adultery: But I say unto you, That whosoever looketh on a woman to lust after her hath committed adultery with her already in his heart." Matthew 5:27, 28.

And what can be said for the women who dress in such a way that they stimulate this kind of thinking? They are equally guilty before God. For this reason no true Christian woman, who understands the effect of such a course, will wear the revealing clothes which create such illicit desires. As the dress inches above the knee, the climate of sin is created. For the carnal man, who has not the power of the gospel in his life, there is no chance whatever to resist the temptation. Every miniskirt is fuel which triggers the mind to think the most debased thoughts of which the carnal nature is capable. Christian women should have no share in this kind of enticement.

Indeed, the second greatest commandment of Jesus would be violated by such a course. Christ said, "Thou shalt love thy neighbor as thyself." How could a woman wear clothing that was designed to cause her neighbor's husband to commit mental adultery, and not be guilty of breaking that law of love? Would she love her neighbor as herself if she willfully did something to cause her neighbor's husband to sin against his wife and against God?

We are dealing here with actions which cause others to sin. Moral issues are directly involved. We are counseled to close every door of temptation.

"Our example and influence must be a power on the side of reform. We must abstain from any practice which will blunt the conscience or encourage temptation. We must open no door that will give Satan access to the mind of one human being formed in the image of God." *Testimonies for the Church*, Vol. 5, p. 360.

Because the female reaction to nudity is so different from that of the male, women often minimize the spiritual problem we are talking about here. Too often their attitude is that men just ought to use more power of self-control and stifle their mental images. They fail completely to grasp the significant difference which God Himself put into the male nature. That nature cannot be reversed by any human effort or determination. It can be controlled by complete Christian commitment, but Christian women must cooperate in closing the avenues of the soul to temptation.

"Our only safety is to be shielded by the grace of God every moment, and not put out our own spiritual eyesight so that we will call evil good, and good, evil. Without hesitation or argument, we must close and guard the avenues of the soul against evil. It will cost us an effort to secure eternal life. It is only by long and per-severing effort, sore discipline, and stern conflict, that we shall be overcomers." *Testimonies for the Church*, Vol. 3, p. 324.

Perhaps we can better understand Satan's way of operating today if we remember some of his classic maneuvers in the past. In 1 Corinthians 10 we read that the experiences of ancient Israel were written for our admonition and example. Reference is made to their leaving Egypt, journeying through the wilderness, and entering the promised land. There is a direct parallel between God's people then and God's people today.

We cannot ignore the fact that Satan's final, win-or-lose-all attack against Israel to keep them from entering the promised land involved the illicit interlude at Baalpeor. The amoral pagan women of Moab swarmed into the camp of Israel with breezy abandon and caused thousands of the men of Israel to fall into sin. God described the scene thus: "For they vex you with their wiles wherewith they have beguiled you in the matter of Peor." Numbers 25:18.

Is there not a striking parallel with the way Satan is seeking to keep modern Israel from entering the heavenly Canaan? Through the wiles of sexual license stirred up by brazen nudity, a last-ditch effort has already been launched to subvert the moral integrity of the remnant church. In the judgment plague which swept the camp of the Israelites, 24,000 died—24,000 men who were overwhelmed by the exotic beauty of the seductive women, and lost the privilege of entering the promised land.

How many thousands of God's people today will be enamored and destroyed by a duplication of such fleshly lusts? Paul, after reviewing the tragic scene at Baalpeor made this appeal: "Now all these things happened unto them for ensamples: and they are written for our admonition upon whom the ends of the world are come. Wherefore let him that thinketh he standeth take heed lest he fall." 1 Corinthians 10:11, 12.

Not one man or woman can boast of any great strength against the pervasive glamour of this worldly age. Just as the senses were captivated by the invading beauties of Moab in the camp of Israel, so the homes of modern Israel are being invaded by the dazzling allure of full-color televised nudity and carnality. Many who think they are standing are sadly compromised already and do not even recognize it.

The undress parade of the latest styles and fashions have also breached the spiritual defenses of many in the church. Only time and eternity will reveal how many minds have surrendered to the sensual appeal of immodest clothing. We wonder if Baalpeor could have been any more bold in its deliberate assault on the morals of Israel. Note the public boast of Mary Quant, the inventor of the miniskirt. This fashion designer declared that her creation was for the purpose of making sex (illicit) more available in the afternoon. In an interview she was asked what kind of person today's woman wants to be, and she answered, "A sexual creature. She displays her sexuality instead of this coy business of hiding it. Today she dresses to say, 'I am sexy. I like men. I enjoy life.'" Then she made this bold statement: "Miniclothes are symbolic of those girls who want to seduce a man."

We think the Israelites were naive and stupid to fall for Balaam's clever sexual intrigue in days of old, but what can we say for the thousands of Seventh-day Adventist women who blithely donned their miniskirts in the face of Mary Quant's confession?

One of the first evidences of Satan-control is the taking off of the clothes. We have proof of that in Luke 8 where the poor demonfilled man was chained in the Gadarene graveyard. The Bible describes him as "a certain man, which had devils long time and ware no clothes." Luke 8:27. Later, when he had been delivered of the legion of evil spirits, he is described as "sitting at the feet of Jesus, clothed, and in his right mind." Verse 35. Evidently his first act upon being set free from Satan's power was to clothe himself again. And the clear implication is that only people not in their right minds would go around without clothes.

Can we conclude that the mass craze for nudity may be based upon modem devil possession? Do the statistics of mental and emotional sickness not support the conclusion also that great numbers of people are not really in their right minds? And these people are being exploited today by Hollywood promoters, smut writers, lewd cultists, and weird designers. They threaten to strip away all modesty and decency from humanity. Their devilish productions constitute a burning insult to the modesty of the human race.

Paul Harvey, noted newspaper columnist, cited the alarming coincidence of crime statistics and short skirts. FBI crime files reveal that forcible rape shot upward almost in proportion to the rise of the hemline. The consensus of law enforcement officers in 50 states agreed that there is a correlation between the miniskirt and sex crimes. Of the law enforcement officers who responded to the question, "Does the short skirt invite sex crimes?" Ninety-one percent answered in the affirmative. The view was summed up by the juvenile division commander of one large city when he said, "Some sex crimes are committed by individuals aroused by their sensory perception, and short dresses of some girls could provoke such an attack."

A newspaper article from Toronto, Canada, confirms that Canadian police agree with the U.S. report: " '91 percent of Toronto policemen think a woman in a revealing miniskirt is more likely to be a rape victim than is her more modest sister,' a spokesman from the Toronto force said Tuesday. Since 1964, the year the mini was introduced to the female fashion market, rapes have increased by 68 percent in the U.S. and by 90 percent in England," said *The Law Officers*, a police publication. "Abbreviated costumes are no doubt a factor in offences against women," said Sgt. George Gough of Toronto's Morality Squad. "When a girl in a short skirt is followed by a man after she gets off a street car at night, there isn't much doubt as to what attracted her assailant."

Dr. Luchenstein, physician at Tombs Prison in New York City, worked with 170,000 prisoners over a twelve-year period. He said, "The so-called crimes of passion are increasing alarmingly, and will continue to do so...until the principal cause is eliminated. This, it seems to me, is the present style of dress, which, to say the least, is immodest. Immodest dress has a direct bearing on crime incitation, no matter how innocent the wearer may be."

Lest any should conclude from this data that the male of the human species is the pawn of uncontrollable urges, let me hasten to say that every individual remains accountable to God on the basis of personal decision. Each man carries the responsibility of sovereign judgment and willful choice, providing no excuse for transgression of God's law.

Finally, we stand or fall not because of the force of temptation, but by the deliberate action of the mind to obey the truth or reject it. The influence of provocative dress habitually prevails over the mind which is not fortified with the Holy Spirit.

DOUBLE STANDARD EXPOSED

No discussion of modest dress would be complete without touch ing on the touchy subject of mixed swimming. Only in this area is the miniskirt almost modest by comparison. Here, by the way, we also discover the blind spot in Adventist dress standards. For some strange reason very little has been said or written on this glaring inconsistency in dealing with our young people. While we take only a soft, rule-book type of stand on miniskirts, we have taken no official stand at all on the matter of mixed swimming. And even the unofficial views of most of the ministry and members do not seem to bear any consistent correlation with the historic principles we have espoused as a church.

Although swimming is one of the finest kinds of recreational activity, the modem bathing suit covers much less of the body than the skimpiest microminiskirt. In truth, very little is left to the imagination. If we condemn the miniskirt, if we endorse any kind of modest dress principle, no matter how vague, how could we by any stretch of the imagination condone a bathing suit as acceptable Christian apparel? Surely no one is so blind as to miss this point. Our young people are not blind, and this is one of the reasons they seem not to listen anymore when we talk to them about modesty. They see the double standard that is being practiced.

It is common practice in our academies to include admonitions in our handbook about modest dress. After that, there may be much or little said about the length of dresses, including low necks, bare backs, and sleevelessness. But in practically all our schools, sometime during the year, the students and teachers go out to some waterfront location, and spend the day playing together in less clothing than is worn by prostitutes who walk the city streets. In fact, if those students and teachers should walk down the main street of any small town wearing their bathing suits they would be refused admission to most business places. They would scandalize even the unconverted community, and risk possible arrest for indecent exposure. *And yet we have blindly accepted this kind of dress as suitable for Seventh-day Adventist Christians to wear in mixed company.* It is ironic that what the world calls indecent in one location, the church would call modest at another location. Does this make any kind of sense? The place has nothing to do with it—it is the principle. The principle against exposing the body applies on the street, the beach, or in the shopping center.

If you want a shocking example of how this creeping compromise has reduced us to the level of the world around us, take a census of the most popular public beaches in July and August. Thousands of Seventh-day Adventists will be mingling with the vulgar multitude. And by the way, you will find no way to identify them from the half-clothed atheists, harlots, and thieves who frequent those resorts. All the flesh looks the same. Does the ocean-front location make it modest to shed our clothes? Do we believe that principles of modesty should be applied only at certain times and places? Are male responses to female nudity somehow thrown out of gear during beach parties and swimming socials?

I have found many of our members who have asked themselves the same questions, but because no one else seemed to be questioning the activity they went along without saying anything. The general feeling seemed to be that the end probably justifies the means in this case. They are getting fine exercise and having a good time.

Others have rationalized that because everyone is in the same state of undress, no one is allowing a big bad thought to come into the head. Also, they get so accustomed to seeing one another half naked that they no longer respond to it. These arguments are not only shallow, but they are untrue. If they were true, then we would have a great case for joining the nudist colony.

My convictions against mixed swimming grew in me as I observed the fruits of the practice. As a young intern-minister in Florida, my assignment in one beachside city was to chaperone the youth at their swimming party. I was astounded to see how inhibitions were lowered by the promiscuous mingling of boys and girls in their bathing suits. Physical liberties were taken, and undue familiarities appeared during the games which were played both in and out of the water. I shall never forget one thing I saw that day. It shocked me into taking my first stand against mixed swimming. One of the lady chaperones climbed up on the shoulders of one of the men who was also helping to supervise the activities. She was one of the spiritual leaders in the church and he was a deacon. Her modesty on Sabbath morning was always exemplary. If a breeze should have lifted her skirt even slightly to expose a knee she would have been embarrassed. Yet, I watched in amazement as she sat astride the shoulders of a man who was not her husband, and rode him around in the water, shrieking with laughter, clad in a scanty bathing suit. She seemed to have no sense whatsoever of the impropriety of what she was doing.

Right then I decided that if this was the effect of mixed swimming I would have to take the position that it was wrong. During the thirty years since that day, I have seen nothing which has changed my feelings about its evil influence.

A while ago I was asked to present these principles of modest dress at a camp meeting. After the meeting, which had occupied two hours in the main auditorium, five young people were waiting to talk to me. The three girls and two boys, all college age, were quite upset by what I had said. The beautiful girl, who seemed to be speaking for all the others, was especially vehement. She said, "How can you say mixed swimming is wrong? We have spent this whole summer with a witnessing team on the Ocean City beach. We spent most of the time in bathing suits, giving Bible studies to other young people on the boardwalk. And this is Tom whom we met there, and he is to be baptized next Sabbath. How can you say we did wrong when we were able to win him for Christ on the beach?"

I expressed joy for the young man who was to be baptized, and commended them for leading him to Christ. Then I asked Tom this question: "Tom, in your association with these girls on the beach in their bathing suits, did you ever find evil or impure thoughts coming into your mind because of the way they were dressed?" Tom dropped his head for just a moment, and then answered, "Yes, of course I did." Immediately the girls chorused their dismay. "Why didn't you tell us then?" one of them asked. They seemed genuinely surprised that the boys had not come up to them at the beach to tell them their suits were provocative.

They went away that day wiser young women, but do you think they forthwith gave up their custom of mixed bathing? I have found that in most cases the ladies do not change their dress styles even after learning how detrimental their influence. The goddess of fashion is a tyrant ruler, and few are committed enough to yield their darling indulgences, especially when the attire caters to the self nature. Dr. Harold Shryock gives this counsel to young dating couples:

"Avoid mixed swimming. Swimming of itself is a wholesome recreation. But when members of both sexes swim together there is introduced an element of personal display which, for any normal human being, directs the thoughts toward the physical characteristics peculiar to the opposite sex. The effort of mixed swimming is to make commonplace those considerations that, for the Christian, are sacred. Mixed swimming tends to lower personal standards of decorum, making physical familiarity seem less objectionable." *The Youth's Instructor*, July 19, 1960.

In the March 1971 issue of *Ministry* magazine a letter to the editor was printed which is worthy of wide distribution. The letter was written by Elder Don Hawley, editor of *Life and Health* magazine.

"In the January, 1970, issue of the *Ministry*, one of our ministers wrote concerning the matter of modesty. He pointed out that our criticism of the miniskirt did not seem to correlate with our complete lack of concern about mixed bathing. He, along with the editors, asked that others express their opinion on the subject, but there has followed a strange silence.

"Is it possible that we know intuitively that mixed bathing is not proper, but since it is so universally practiced by the church it seems best to ignore the situation? If so, this is a 'head in the sand' approach. No matter how universal some impropriety may be, we still have to answer individually in the judgment.

"Perhaps there were those who did have convictions, but who felt it would not be politically expedient to express them. I once heard a conference president downgrade a particular pastor because 'he's rather fanatical; he doesn't believe in mixed bathing.'

"We decry the wearing of shorts, the backless back, and plunging neckline, and the miniskirt, pointing out that such people are 'half naked.' But if that person switches to a condition of being three quarters naked (i.e. into swim wear), then all is well. Apparently if we want to do something badly enough, such as engage in mixed swimming, then the laws of modesty can be temporarily abrogated.

"Until a few years ago at least, a person leaving a public beach in swimming attire and walking a block to a shopping area, would risk arrest for 'indecent exposure.' Isn't it a bit strange that what the world labels indecent, the church finds acceptable?

"In one conference the following regulations are in force during campmeeting: 'Swimmers are requested to use bathing caps and to be properly and modestly dressed going to and from the pool. Street clothes or bathing robes are required.' Think about this for a moment. The unavoidable inference is that once one gets to the pool, it will be all right to wear only bathing attire and be immodestly dressed...."

Some have asked whether E. G. White spoke on the subject of mixed bathing. According to the White Estate there is no record of such counsel. Obviously, the wearing of bikinis and skimpy bathing suits was not any problem under the Victorian aura of the mid-1800s.

When I wrote for information on the subject from the White Estate, they sent me a copy of a letter which had been written to someone who had made a similar inquiry. The secretary of the Estate wrote the letter December 8, 1953:

"The question of mixed bathing about which you wrote sometime ago is certainly a most difficult one to deal with under present day conditions. Unfortunately we have not a single statement in the writings of Ellen G. White in which the subject is mentioned directly. Conclusions must be based on principles stated in the Bible and the Spirit of Prophecy rather than on any specific bit of instruction. Of course, this is true of many other subjects concerning which we must make decisions regularly. You asked about my convictions on the matter, so I shall pass them on with some of the statements of principles involved in reaching the conclusions.

"In dealing with a good many hundreds of young people during the years of my teaching, I have discovered what you have also found—that, while it may be difficult to hold the line regarding some standards and activities, it is easier to hold than to back up after yielding to pressure to follow a course of action that is not clearly a right one. So far as I can learn, our colleges that have pools are still holding to separate periods for swimming. That is the position recommended by our Missionary Volunteer Department, and I believe the position is a sound one.

"You may be interested to know that the Missionary Volunteer Advisory Council, in its meeting just preceding the recent Autumn Council, emphatically reaffirmed its former position that we should not sponsor groups for mixed bathing. While the action does not specify all of the situations involved, the discussion centered in the church and M.V. Society, the school, and the camp. The men felt that circumstances warrant a strong reaffirmation of this point of view. Their observation has been that where some have not followed this course, most unfortunate results have been obtained.

"You mentioned that our young people are beyond being shocked by anything they might see in connection with a swimming party. I believe that is true of many of them. One of my great questions is whether we as church leaders should sponsor things that will only serve to foster this tendency to be shock-proof. We must admit that repeated exposures to conscience-deadening influences have brought our young people to the condition in which we find them. Is it not our responsibility to do our best to avoid anything that will continue these influences? Rather than there being more reasons today for going ahead with mixed bathing than in the past, it seems that with the increased freedom of association and almost complete lack of inhibitions on the part of young people, the reasons for avoiding more freedom are multiplying.

"So far as the argument is concerned that people are so used to seeing immodesty that immodest bathing suits mean nothing to them, I believe that it is entirely fallacious. The Bible instruction is that Christians should be modestly dressed no matter what anyone else does. The fact that many consciences are hardened does not alter basic principles. It would require a rather ingenious individual to invent arguments to prove that the modern version of the bathing suit is 'modest apparel.' While many refuse to admit it, for boys and men to be in close association with girls and women in the near state of nudity that the current bathing suit encourages is a very real source of temptation. All one needs to do is to take a glance at some of the advertising matter for women's bathing suits, to discover that it is the studied purpose of the manufacturers to focus male attention on the female form. For the church to encourage association on this basis is not a soul-winning endeavor.

"While it is true that many young people, especially the teenagers, consider us unrealistic in our approach to matters of this sort, that is not a new attitude. My contact with history has left me with the distinct impression that every generation of young people has considered its elders hopelessly out of date. As Christian parents and leaders, God has left it in our hands to teach our youth in such a way that, while they may not fully agree with us at present, the time will come when they will see the wisdom of our course. I have had many young people in later years thank me for prohibitions against which they chafed when they first encountered them.

"You mentioned that those who are interested in swimming parties do not support the other social activities of the church. However, if you should inaugurate church sponsored swims, most of these individuals would still not support anything but the swims. They would not immediately gain interest in the other activities just because you had yielded to their urging in this matter.

"All this may sound as if I am one of those 'ridiculously unrealistic' persons of whom the young people speak. I assure you that this is not so. It is just that I have lived with young people every day for so many years that I have become exceedingly aware of the results when we yield to some of their unwise urgings. These days we need to place before our young people every incentive for right thinking and acting. Mixed bathing is not such an incentive.

"Swimming is one of the best of all exercises, and certainly it is a proper physical activity for Christians when engaged in moderation and under the proper circumstances. If it is the physical benefit that is desired, this object can be gained by our sponsoring swims for young men and young women separately in appropriate places. I greatly miss the opportunity to go swimming as frequently as I would like, because of the difficulty of finding suitable places for the recreation. I know many others who feel the same way, but our young people must learn to take a proper attitude toward denying present pleasures for future benefits.

"I sympathize with you in your problem. It is a perennial one in our schools, and I have been trying to cope with it for a dozen years. It seems to me that this is something that must be left as a decision for families to make. If consecrated parents decide that they wish to accompany their children as a family or as a group of families, certainly we should not condemn them, but for the church to sponsor swimming parties of this kind is an entirely different matter."

UNISEX

Any discussion of dress today would be incomplete without some consideration being given to the topic of unisex. One of the phenomena of our times is the mushrooming growth of look-alike boutiques and hair salons. Unisex shops and signs are appearing all across the country offering exactly the same clothes and hairdos to both men and women. What is the significance of this development? Are there any spiritual dangers inherent in this growing trend?

First, we need to take note of the astronomical rise in homosexuality in the last few years. America has been literally swamped in a blitz of newspaper and magazine stories about the gay movement, and how it has proudly come out of the closet to demand its rights. Gay marches and demonstrations attract great crowds and wide publicity. Television forums have openly discussed the matter before millions of viewers, with both lesbians and homosexuals taking part.

Psychiatry has given formal recognition to the practice as normal sex behavior. Great Protestant church organizations are not only opening the doors to membership, but are ordaining self-professed homosexuals to the ministry. Churches have been established exclusively for the worship of homosexuals, and some marriages have been performed and publicly registered between two persons of the same sex.

Much has been written about the possible causes for this spectacular escalation of a very old perversion. Very few seem to understand exactly why it has made such a sudden resurgence, but I believe we can discover the reasons by examining some parallel social developments which have given explicit encouragement to the gay movement. There is a cause for every effect, and through the centuries of time the same conditions have produced similar results.

All Bible students are acquainted with the strong condemnation of sodomy which is woven throughout both Old and New Testaments. God labels it as one of the worst abominations, a sin which will utterly deprave and destroy. The ancient pagan world was riddled with the vice. The very name is derived from the city of Sodom which harbored a host of militant homosexuals. Paul speaks in Romans 1:26 and 27 of "vile affections: for even their women did change the natural use into that which is against nature: And likewise also the men, leaving the natural use of the woman, burned in their lust one toward another; men with men working that which is unseemly, and receiving in themselves that recompense of their error which was meet." The reprobate minds "which commit such things are worthy of death," Paul stated in verse 32.

The land of Canaan, which the Israelites were to possess, was filled with the perverse iniquity of sodomy or homosexuality. This was one of the reasons God gave such explicit instructions for them not to intermarry or intermingle with the inhabitants of the land. They were to avoid any contaminating contact which could lead Israel to join their debased practices. Furthermore, they were given specific instructions against dressing in a way that could create the climate for committing this sin. "The woman shall not wear that which pertaineth unto a man, neither shall a man put on a woman's garment: for all that do so are abomination unto the Lord thy God." Deuteronomy 22:5.

Because sodomy involves a changing of sex roles which is usually accompanied by a pattern of acting and dressing like the opposite sex, God warned His people not to open any door of temptation on this matter. They were to maintain clear lines of distinction between the dress of men and women. The New Testament reaffirms this principle of separation in appearance. Paul wrote, "Doth not even nature itself teach you that, if a man have long hair, it is a shame unto him? But if a woman have long hair, it is a glory to her." 1 Corinthians 11:14, 15.

Now we are ready to make some observations about the modern social scene which could explain why we see the alarming rise of homosexuality. If God saw that the blurring of sexual identity could cause problems, then we must admit to having a great problem. We are seeing three factors at work today which have never operated before in human history at the same time.. Taken alone, none of these three things would be too impressive. But when we see the combined effect of their influence, it is frightening even to contemplate. The three contemporary conditions are these:

(1) The Women's Lib Movement, whose declared purpose is to interchange the roles of men and women in much of our social, economic, and religious life.

(2) The pantsuit fashion revolution, which has led the majority of women to abandon the traditional feminine dress styles.

(3) The growing tendency of men to dress in frills, with feminine hair styles, and accompanying demasculinization.

This combination of related circumstances has probably been responsible for pushing thousands of borderline homosexuals over the line into perversion. Many of them only needed the little bit of psychotic confusion that the three popular movements thrust upon them.

Dr. Charles Winick, professor of Sociology at the City University of New York, is one leading authority who feels that the current vogue for interchangeable clothing is leading us to ultimate disaster. In his provocative book, *The New People*, he delineates the numerous ways that unisex is desexualizing the American people. He believes that even the over-thirty group has been critically affected by the radical changes around them, although they don't fully realize how it is happening.

Dr. Winick points out that even the staid business men are edging into patterned, pastel-hued shirts and pants. Men's departments are doing a brisk business in jewelry, scented grooming aids, hair pieces, manicures, face creams, and colognes. Hair nets and permanent waves are discreetly labeled with terms like "trainers" and "hair processing."

In his book Dr. Winick catalogues several hundred pages of items in our culture that have become neutralized, bland, and consequently boring. For example: Parents are giving more and more interchangeable names to their children such as Kim, Chris, Leslie, Gene, Lee, and Dana. He believes that the blurring of masculine and feminine distinctions is leading our society into deep trouble, because people cannot cope with critical life situations until they are certain of their sexual identity. Unisex clothing is confusing them and creating serious emotional crises for many. Sociologist Winick doesn't care how masculinity and femininity are defined as long as they are clearly defined. "Just about every combination of male and female role-relationships can be healthy and effective except one in which roles are blurred," he wrote in *Medical Opinion and Review*, a magazine for physicians.

With both Bible writers and social experts focusing on unisex clothing as a factor in creating sexual confusion, what should be our own personal attitude toward this spreading vogue? As members of the remnant church we have not been left without guidance on the matter. E. G. White commented on the biblical position in these words:

"I was referred to Deuteronomy 22:5: 'The woman shall not wear that which pertaineth unto a man, neither shall a man put on a woman's garment, for all that do so are an abomination unto the Lord thy God.'...There is an increasing tendency to have women in their dress and appearance as near like the other sex as possible, and to fashion their dress very much like that of men, but God pronounces it abomination." *Testimonies for the Church*, Vol. 1, p. 457.

Please notice that she called it abomination for women to fashion their dress much like that of men. So the issue for us is no longer whether the clothes are actually those of the opposite sex. They might be created for one sex only, but be fashioned like the opposite sex. Thus the influence could be to push the bisexuals or fringe homosexuals over the line into the confirmed camp.

Now the question is raised: Where should the line be drawn between male and female styles of clothing? There seems to be no disagreement about wearing the actual clothing of the opposite sex. It is clearly forbidden. There is apparently much disagreement about the degree of similarity which can exist without becoming an abomination.

Many are convinced that the typical pantsuit is already fashioned very much after that of men. But if it is not, how many small changes would it take to put it into the category of being so fashioned? At that point Mrs. White said it would be an abomination. As the pantsuit collars widen and coat styles shift to become more and more masculine, would it be possible to detect the point of transition from stylish to abomination?

Each month as the popular pantsuits adapt slightly more to the unisex, Adventist women continue to buy theirs from the styles available. Finally, one small change could place them in the category of being "fashioned very much like that of men." In harmony with his last-day strategy of creeping in by degrees, Satan could lead the remnant church into the unisex camp just as he led so many into the miniskirt scandal. And it would be done in such a way that few would recognize where the little steps were leading. Remember the small hoops of Sister A? In the same innocuous manner the pantsuits of women and the effeminate styles of men could bring weakness and shame to the remnant church.

Many sincere Adventists believe that the Spirit of Prophecy condones the pantsuit fashions. The truth is that Mrs. White took the opposite position. She condemned it. The popular American costume of Mrs. White's day is described by her in these words: "It consists of a vest, pants, and a dress resembling a coat and reaching about halfway from the hip to the knee. This dress I have opposed, from what has been shown me, as not in harmony with the Word of God." *Testimonies for the Church*, Vol 1, p. 465.

In what respect does that dress differ from the modern pantsuit? She was describing almost exactly what we see being worn by the vast majority of women today, except that the dress coat is a bit shorter on today's version. Later Mrs. White described the objections to that particular dress which made it unacceptable. She saw in vision three companies of ladies pass before her. The second group was wearing the dress which she described as the American Costume. Here are her comments: "The dress of the second class which passed before me was in many respects as it should be. The limbs were well clad. They were free from the burdens which the tyrant, Fashion, had imposed upon the first class; but had gone to that extreme in the short dress as to disgust and prejudice good people, and destroy in a great measure their own influence. This is the style and influence of the 'American Costume' taught and worn by many at 'Our Home' in Dansville, New York. It does not reach to the knee. I need not say that this style of dress was shown me to be too short." *Present Truth and Review and Herald Articles*, Vol. 1, p. 73.

Now the picture comes into clear focus. The dress which was described as "vest (blouse), pants, and a dress resembling a coat and reaching about halfway from the hip to the knee" was not acceptable because the dress did not reach to the knees. In other words, pants apparently were not objectionable if they were covered by a dress which came at least to the knees. This, of course, pantsuits do not do. So we have no reason to conclude that she would approve of today's version of the American Costume, the pantsuit. She clearly stated "I saw that God's order has been reversed, and His special directions disregarded, by those who adopt the American Costume. I was referred to Deuteronomy 22:5." *Testimonies for the Church*, Vol. 1, p. 457.

It is true that some of the pantsuit blouses are distinctly feminine in their cut and style, while others are severely masculine. Many fine Christian women defend the wearing of the feminine type, and others who are just as dedicated see no harm in wearing the more masculine. It is not the purpose of this study to designate some line between these two fashions which separate wrong from right.

No one, as far as I can tell, would know where such a line should be drawn. Every Adventist sister should weigh the dangers involved in taking the first step that would encourage a unisex trend. Those tiny steps which Satan uses to lead into the snare are often so innocent that they can be defended with righteous enthusiasm.

It is truly difficult to debate the argument that pantsuits are more modest than many current dress styles. But in the light of our knowledge about Satan's "modus operandi" and the lesson of the good wheat and quails, we should ask, Where would it lead us? Would it be a step closer to the abomination that Mrs. White referred to? And would it give encouragement to Sister B to make her pantsuit just a little more mannish? And what about Sister C, who would go a step further?—and they, along with every other lady who wears them, all the while protesting they are not wearing masculine clothes at all.

COLORFUL COSMETICS AND JEWELRY

One of the most frequent and mistaken complaints that people make against religion is that it is too restrictive. In this permissive age when all the emphasis seems to be upon "doing your own thing," an unreasonable attitude of self-will has developed. This attitude has even intruded into religion. Church members and nonmembers seem to be in quest of the same thing: a religion which doesn't interfere with personal rights and freedom. Suspicion is aroused instantly against any doctrine which demands the "giving up" of anything.

As this liberal spirit has grown stronger, many church members have turned more and more critical of the high spiritual standards upheld by the church. Obviously embarrassed by the widening gap between the church and the world, and unwilling to meet the social stigma of being a "peculiar" minority, these members have sought to justify their compromise in the area of Christian standards. They often argue that the church is being narrow and legalistic and that many fine people are being discouraged from joining the church by this "arbitrary imposition of rules."

If these complaints are valid, then some basic changes surely need to be made in the doctrine of the church. If they are not valid, then we desperately need to know how to present the standards of Christian conduct in their true biblical setting. In other words, we must definitely establish whether these rules were made by God or by the church. We must also find out if they are arbitrary prohibitions or God's loving regulations for our own happiness.

In contrast to the popular revolt against any absolute law of individual conduct, we must consider the Bible facts about the Christian life in general and morals in particular. How compatible are these modern demands for personal freedom with the standards of God's Word? Let us suppose that the true biblical position could be presented with all the love and persuasion of an angel from Heaven. Would the truth be easy for anyone to accept?

Let's face it. The path to eternal life is not a soft, flowery way of ease. Jesus laid such emphasis upon this in so many texts that we cannot be blind to it. He said, "Strait is the gate, and narrow is the way, which leadeth unto life, and few there be that find it." Matthew 7:14. One of the very first principles of being a Christian is self denial. Christ said, "If any man will come after me, let him deny himself, and take up his cross daily, and follow me." Luke 9:23. To be a Christian involves complete surrender. Our Lord's parable of the pearl and the merchantman reveals that we must be willing to invest every single thing we have in obtaining that tremendous prize of eternal life. If we allow one thing or one person to come between us and doing the will of Christ, we cannot be saved.

Have we been guilty of discounting the price of discipleship so that people will not feel that the path is too narrow and restrictive? Jesus said, "Whosoever he be of you that forsaketh not all that he hath, he cannot be my disciple." Luke 14:33. The rich young ruler was told by Jesus that he lacked only one thing in his preparation for Heaven, but that one thing he was not willing to do. He would have to surrender his wealth in order to be saved, but he was not willing to give it away. He loved something more than he loved the Lord, and he went away sorrowful and lost. The position of Christ was so strong on this point that He even said, "He that loveth father or mother more than me is not worthy of me: and he that loveth son or daughter more than me is not worthy of me." Matthew 10:37.

Now, I believe that we should search for the kindest, most tactful and loving way to present the claims of Christ to men and women. But I also believe that it will make little difference how it is presented, if individuals have no love for the Lord Jesus. The fault does not lie with the message; some of the fault lies with the preachers in the way they present it, but much of the fault lies in the attitude of the complaining Christian who feels rebellious against the truth because it requires a degree of self-denial.

Let me illustrate how personal feelings and attitude can make all the difference in the world. Marriage is the most restrictive experience that any human being can voluntarily assume in this world, aside from his spiritual commitment to Christ. The man promises to surrender many of his former attachments and practices. He yields up his freedom to date other girls, and solemnly binds himself to that one-and-only for the rest of his life. The bride also makes similar restrictive pledges, and agrees to forsake all others in her devotion to the man at her side. The wedding vows are undoubtedly among the most narrow, rigid commitments any human being can make in his lifetime. If restrictions and rules are the cause of so much misery, then weddings should be the most miserable, unhappy experiences for all concerned. But not so! They are the happiest events. Why? Why is the bride so radiant as she stands up to pledge her very life away to the groom? How can the man be so happy to make the promises which will inhibit his activities for the rest of his life? The answer is simple. They love each other. It is their attitude and feeling toward each other that makes the restrictions a joy to accept.

Have you ever heard a bride complaining after the ceremony? Probably no one has ever heard her say bitterly, "Now I can't date Jim and Andy anymore. It's not fair. The State is forcing me to be faithful to my husband. This marriage business is too restrictive." No, you've not heard that. Neither have you heard a new bridegroom complaining that he is now compelled to give part of his salary to support his wife. True, the law demands that he do it under penalty of imprisonment, but he is not even conscious of the law. State law is ready to convict the bride if she commits adultery, but she doesn't even think of such a law. They are in love, and love changes everything. They are not being faithful because of fear of punishment. They are being faithful because they want to please the person whom they love so deeply.

The most miserable men and women in this world are the ones who are married and no longer love each other. Here is almost literally hell on earth. They chafe and complain about the restrictions and impositions upon them. Similarly, the unhappiest church members in all the world are those who are married to Christ through baptism, and yet do not love Him. They are often bitterly blaming the church and their instructors for imposing upon them their narrow, restrictive religion.

But is it the religion or the pastors who are at fault? The sad fact is that those people have never entered the personal love-relationship which is the cornerstone of all true religion. Many of them have learned the right texts for the Bible study course and are quite able to explain the order of last-day events, but they have had no personal encounter with Jesus Christ. Somewhere, and perhaps everywhere, along the lines of the indoctrination they were not taught, or did not choose to accept, the true basis of heart religion. It is not a set of rules or a list of doctrines, but a deeply personal involvement in a love affair with the man Jesus Christ.

The difficulty with millions of Christians is their motive for being church members. They have a fire-escape religion. They do certain things only because they are afraid of the fire at the end of the road. They serve the Lord fearfully because they tremble at the thought of being cast into the lake of fire. No wonder they are longfaced and miserable! What a perversion of the truth! Christians should be the happiest people in the world—happier even than the newlyweds as they leave the wedding chapel! The Christian should love the Lord even more than husband or wife.

Do you think a home could be happy if the wife prepared her husband's favorite dish each day because she feared he might divorce her?

Earthly relationships would collapse under this strain. She prepares that dish because she loves her husband and wants to please him. When his wife's birthday approaches, a loving, Christian husband often watches and listens for an indication of what his wife would like to have. And usually she doesn't have to hit him over the head to let him know! He gladly buys her the gift because he loves her and wants to please her. In the same way the Christian will be searching the Bible daily to discover ways of pleasing the Lord. He will constantly be looking for signs and indications of how to please the One he loves supremely. In the Twentieth Century translation of the Bible we read these words, "Always be trying to find out what best pleases the Lord." Ephesians 5:10. What a motto for every Christian! Indeed this is the supreme desire of those who love the Lord sincerely. No wonder Christ summarized the first table of the law in these words: "Thou shalt love the Lord thy God with all thy heart, and with all thy soul, and with all thy mind. This is the first and great commandment." Matthew 22:37, 38.

The real reason some Christians chafe and complain about the rules and the strictness is because they have only enough religion to make them miserable. The scope of their Christian "experience" is based upon a constant struggle to live up to the rules—an effort to keep the law. Now certainly there is nothing wrong with obeying the commandments of God any more than there is with a husband obeying the state law to support his wife. But if the demands of the law are the only reason for obeying it, then something is seriously wrong with the Christian and with the husband. Love lifts the legal load and makes delightful what could be a burden and strain.

A mother of three boys was having a terrible struggle trying to enforce the laws of good grooming and cleanliness. Like most little boys these three resisted the rules about washing ears, combing hair, and shining shoes. It was a daily battle which Mother won only through the long arm of authority and force. But one day the oldest boy, in his early teens, walked out of his room looking the model of impeccable neatness. Every hair seemed to be in exactly the right place, and the shoes below the well-turned cuff were shining to perfection. The mother almost fainted. Hardly able to suppress her surprise and delight, she wisely decided to wait and watch for the answer to this turn of events. The solution to the puzzle was not long in coming. The very next day Mother learned that a new family had moved in down the block, and there was a girl in the family. Perhaps the girl had not seen Johnny, but he had already seen her and it had profoundly affected him. We'll not say that it was love which changed his attitude toward the laws of good grooming, but he definitely wasn't cleaning up from fear of mother's enforcement any longer.

The point is that the Christian life is not composed of just "do's" and "don'ts." There are restrictions, to be sure, in this spiritual marriage, just as there are in physical marriage. But those restrictions are imposed by love which seeks always and ever to please the object of the affections. Those Christians who are in love with Christ are exuberant, beaming witnesses that this is the way of true happiness. Unfortunately, there is a larger group of church members who are miserably enduring what should be blissfully enjoyed. They are bitter and complaining about not being able to eat what they please or dress as they wish to. They blame the church for their being forced to "give up" so many things. Their religion seems much like the man with a headache. He didn't want to cut off his head but it hurt him to keep it. Their joyless attitude seems to assume that their religion is the product of some committee of gloomy preachers bent on including all the prohibitive rules that could make men, women, and young people unhappy.

But is this true? What about the spiritual principles which make up the doctrine which we call Christian standards? Is it an arbitrary church law that one should not attend the theater? Is it God's decision or man's decision that dancing is improper for a Christian? And what about the use of colorful cosmetics and jewelry—is it pleasing to God or displeasing? The truth is that every point of our faith and doctrine should be based soundly upon the principle of doing God's will as revealed in the Bible. Love for Him will always provoke the question, how can I always be trying to find out what best pleases the Lord?

The answer to that question is found in scores of Bible texts which give indications and clear signals on how to please Him rather than ourselves. This is the only really relevant question concerning any activity or practice. What does God think about it? It doesn't matter what this preacher or that preacher thinks of it, or what this church or that church believes about it. The great, all-important question is this: Is it pleasing or displeasing to the Lord? If we find texts which reveal that God doesn't approve, there should be no further debate with the genuine Christian. We love Him too much to risk displeasing Him. Our delight should be to find and execute those things that please the One we love, and to eliminate from our lives those things that displease Him.

When people are in love they do not need to threaten each other or lay down ultimatums. They constantly search for ways to show their love and to please one another. Those who fulfill the first and great command of Christ will not feel it a burden to obey. God is searching for those who will be sensitive to the slightest indication of His will. He is not pleased by those who must be constantly prodded into line by fear of punishment. God says: "I will instruct thee and teach thee in the way which thou shalt go: I will guide thee with mine eye. Be ye not as the horse, or as the mule, which have no understanding; whose mouth must be held in with bit and bridle, lest they come near unto thee." Psalm 32:8, 9.

Many Christians are "bit-and-bridle" followers. They respond only to threats, and obey because of fear of punishment. God says, "I want you to be corrected by a look from me." Only those who love Him supremely and are watching for indications of His pleasure will recognize the loving glance of correction. Searching the Bible with one purpose—to discover what pleases Him—they will immediately obey the slightest revelation of His will. *This is the essence of true Christianity—ordering every level of life in harmony with His revealed will, because of love.*

With this little background on how to make love the motivating factor in setting up Christian standards, we are now prepared to illustrate how the principle operates in practice. Although any one of the "conduct" standards of the church could be used, let us choose one which has evoked considerable complaint—colorful cosmetics and jewelry. Multitudes of sincere members have laid aside the use of these artificial adornments "because the church says so." This is a poor reason for doing anything in the Christian life. It is hoped that the reading of this chapter will cause explanations about arbitrary church rules on the subject to give way to personal conviction based on loving and pleasing the Lord.

Repeatedly, pastors have faced the questions: "What is wrong with my little wedding ring? Do you think God will leave me out of Heaven just because I wear this bit of jewelry?" My own heart has been dismayed and troubled on many occasions over this negative approach to Christianity. Please note what the question implies. The questioner is obviously seeking to know how much he can get by with, and still make it to Heaven. His attitude reflects a legalistic desire to do only the things which are laid down as divine "do-it-or-else" laws.

But this approach is wrong, wrong, wrong! The true Christian will not ask, "How much do I have to do in order to remain a child of God?" but rather, "How much can I do to please Jesus whom I love?" This is the positive approach based on seeking God's will on the questions and loving Him enough to obey His will happily as revealed in the Bible. Once this open-hearted, loving premise is accepted it remains only to search through the Scripture to find indications of God's will concerning the use of colorful cosmetics and ornaments. This we shall now proceed to do.

In Genesis 35:1-4, Jacob was told by God to take his family to Bethel where they were to be presented at the altar of the Lord. This was a very sacred spot to Jacob—the place of his conversion in earlier days, after seeing the heavenly ladder in his dream. But before they could be consecrated at that holy spot, Jacob told his household to "put away the strange gods that are among you." Verse 2. Apparently the family had picked up some of the heathen customs in their tarrying in the land. There were certain objects which had to be laid aside before they went up to the altar, because they were pagan objects. Please notice, in verse 4, what these objects were: "And they gave unto Jacob all the strange gods which were in their hand, and all the earrings which were in their ears: and Jacob hid them under the oak which was by Shechem." In Judges 8:24 we are assured that earrings were worn by those who were Ishmaelites. The context strongly implies that they wore the ornaments as a mark of their apostasy from the true God. The thirty-fourth chapter of Genesis reveals that Jacob's sons had committed some grievous sins, and Jacob was coming before God to make a solemn atonement for them and for his family. It was a time of heart-searching and repentance. Everything was done to make wrongs right and to open the way for God's blessing to come upon them. The custom of wearing heathen ornaments was given up, along with the strange gods. The earrings were laid aside.

Under similar circumstances a reformation took place in Exodus 33:1-6. A terrible apostasy had developed in the previous chapter while Moses was in the mountain receiving the Ten Commandments. A large number of the Israelites had worshipped the golden calf, bringing plague and destruction which threatened the nation. Moses called for them to repent in these words: "Consecrate yourselves today to the Lord, even every man upon his son, and upon his brother; that he may bestow upon you a blessing this day." Exodus 32:29.

In the next chapter, Moses went up to the tabernacle to plead with God for the people, who were still adorned with their heathen trappings from the day of indulgence and sin. The instruction God gave for the restoration of Israel included a change of dress, just as it had earlier in the case of Jacob and his family. God said, "Say unto the children of Israel, Ye are a stiffnecked people; I will come up into the midst of thee in a moment, and consume thee: therefore now put off thy ornaments from thee, that I may know what to do unto thee. And the children of Israel stripped themselves of their ornaments by the mount Horeb." Exodus 33:5, 6.

We are left in no doubt as to the attitude of God concerning the wearing of those ornaments. God, who changes not, told them to take off those things and present themselves for judgment, to answer for their apostasy. It is of more than passing interest to note that this prohibition was laid down in connection with their going into the promised land. God said, "I will send an angel before thee; and I will drive out the Canaanite, the Amorite ... for I will not go up in the midst of thee; for thou art a stiffnecked people." Exodus 33:2, 3. It is significant that they were required to strip off the ornaments before they could enter the promised land. Does this have anything to do with us? Indeed it does. Paul assures us in 1 Corinthians 10:11 that "all these things happened unto them for ensamples: and they are written for our admonition, upon whom the ends of the world are come." He likens their Red Sea experience to baptism in verse 2, and in verses 7 and 8 he refers to the great apostasy experience of Israel in Exodus 32, when they made their golden calf. Then immediately he explains in verse 11 that these things which happened to them were for "our admonition." This can only mean that God's dealing with them over their apostasy is to teach us something. His command for them to remove the ornaments before going into the land of Canaan applies to us before going into the heavenly Canaan. The parallel is obvious in the context.

The earliest record in existence concerning the use of colorful cosmetics is found in 2 Kings 9:30. Many have questioned the origin of the expression "painted up like Jezebel." The answer is found in this text. "And when Jehu was come to Jezreel, Jezebel heard of it; and she painted her face, and tired her head, and looked out at a window." The history of that infamous heathen queen, who put hundreds of God's prophets to death, is well known to Bible students. To trace the biblical origin of the custom to Jezebel certainly casts an unholy shadow over the practice. But we shall see in a moment that the use of colorful cosmetics was a consistent mark of heathen women and unfaithful women throughout the Bible record.

Through the prophet Isaiah God sent one of the most scathing denunciations of jewelry that can be found anywhere in the Bible. Nowhere do we find a more direct and unequivocal revelation of God's feelings toward the wearing of ornaments. In Isaiah 3:16 God does not generalize about ornaments, but gives a long list of specific articles which were being worn by the "daughters of Zion." Now, let's notice whether God, the same yesterday, today, and forever, was pleased with the wearing of these things. "Moreover the Lord saith, Because the daughters of Zion are haughty, and walk with stretched forth necks and wanton eyes, walking and mincing as they go, and making a tinkling with their feet...In that day the Lord will take away the bravery of their tinkling ornaments about their feet, and their cauls,...the chains, and the bracelets, and the mufflers,... the ornaments of the legs, and the headbands, and the tablets, and the earrings, the rings, and nose jewels." Isaiah 3:16-21.

Let's pause in the midst of this recital and ask the question, How will God take away these things? In the next chapter, verse 4, we read, "When the Lord shall have washed away the filth of the daughters of Zion...by the spirit of burning." Don't overlook the fact that God refers to all these objects of adornment as "filth." He further describes most graphically the ones who survive the "washing away" of the ornaments: "In that day shall the branch of the Lord be beautiful and glorious, and the fruit of the earth shall be excellent and comely for them that are escaped of Israel. And it shall come to pass, that he that is left in Zion, and he that remaineth in Jerusalem, shall be called holy, even everyone that is written among the living in Jerusalem." Isaiah 4:2, 3.

In bold, clear strokes the prophet reveals the abhorrence of God for the manifestations of pride in wearing ornaments. After the washing away of those artificial baubles, God describes the women as being "comely," "holy," and "beautiful." Apparently He does not appraise beauty in the same way that we do. The women put on all their jewelry to make themselves beautiful, but God said it was filthy. When it was all washed away, He said they were comely and beautiful. Do not miss the extreme significance of this truth. God uses that word "comely" to describe His bride, the church. "I have likened the daughter of Zion to a comely and delicate woman." Jeremiah 6:2.

As if to reinforce His assessment of the type of pride under consideration, God made the following observation: "The shew of their countenance doth witness against them; and they declare their sin as Sodom, they hide it not. Woe unto their soul! for they have rewarded evil unto themselves." Isaiah 3:9. No question is permitted to remain about the impropriety of outward adornment. Their decorated faces were involved in the vanity to such a degree that God used the women's makeup as an example of brazen shamelessness.

It will be well to take note at this point that God identified rings as part of the "filth of the daughters of Zion." What kind of rings was he talking about? High school seniors will answer immediately, "My class ring is symbolic of my being a senior. It's not worn as an ornament. God was talking about other kinds of rings." The Mason will defend his Masonic ring in almost the same words: "God wasn't talking about my ring. It simply represents my belonging to the Lodge." And then there are the birthstone rings, the engagement rings, and the wedding rings—they also have symbolic meanings. How easy to justify the one we happen to be wearing and to claim that God was not talking about that one. But how do we know God wasn't talking about the very one we are wearing? Would it not be presumptuous to feel that God makes an exception for the one we are wearing, just because we don't want to give it up?

After all, why are we searching the Bible on this subject? Are we not trying to find out what best pleases the Lord? We are not seeking for ways to get around what pleases Him. Our sole purpose is to find His will in order to do it. We love Him too much to risk displeasing Him. This is why the true Christian will not quibble over the kind of ring, or seek a rationalization in going contrary to God's will. Lay aside all rings. Isn't it patently obvious that if one symbolic ring can be defended, then all symbolic rings can be defended? In no instance do we find any biblical precedent for wearing a physical sign of marriage. The history of the wedding ring is tainted with pagan sun-worship and papal superstition. Not one argument put forward in its favor carries any weight in comparison to the one great fact that *it is not pleasing to the Lord!* A carnal Christian could argue that it is not clear that one will be lost for wearing a ring. But the Christian who loves God supremely will answer that it is enough to know that it displeases our Lover and Friend.

Incidentally, there is plenty of historic evidence of the pagan origin of the wearing of a wedding ring. John Henry Newman, after he forsook Anglicanism to become, later, a cardinal of the Roman Catholic church, wrote these words: "Constantine, in order to recommend the new religion to the heathen, transferred into it the outward adornments to which they had been accustomed in their own. It is not necessary to go into a subject which the diligence of Protestant writers has made familiar to most of us. The use of temples, and these dedicated to particular saints…incense…candles…holy water…processions…*the ring in marriage*, turning to the east, images at a later date…are all of pagan origin, and sanctified by their adoption into the Church." *An Essay On the Development of Christian Doctrine*, p. 373. (Emphasis supplied.)

The prophet Jeremiah, like so many other Old Testament writers, added more counsel concerning the type of people who wore artificial ornaments. God moved upon those holy men to represent the church prophetically as a woman. When God's people were backslidden, they were portrayed by the prophet as a harlot or an unfaithful wife. Thus we read texts like the following: "And when thou art spoiled, what wilt thou do? Though thou clothest thyself with crimson, though thou deckest thee with ornaments of gold, though thou rentest thy face with painting, in vain shalt thou make thyself fair; thy lovers will despise thee, they will seek thy life." Jeremiah 4:30.

Through Ezekiel, God symbolized His apostatized people, Judah and Israel, by two harlots named Aholah and Aholibah. His description of their bold ornamentation matched the lewdness of their conduct. "And furthermore, that ye have sent for men to come from far, unto whom a messenger was sent; and, lo, they came: for whom thou didst wash thyself, paintedst thy eyes, and deckedst thyself with ornaments." Ezekiel 23:40.

Hosea expresses the same thought when he describes the hypocrisy of Israel. Again, the unfaithfulness was well dramatized by a decorated woman. "And I will visit upon her the days of Baalim, wherein she burned incense to them, and she decked herself with her earrings and her jewels, and she went after her lovers, and forgat me, saith the Lord." Hosea 2:13.

Over and over again, the Bible connects the wearing of colorful cosmetics and jewelry with sin, apostasy, and heathenism. When they turned away from the Lord they put on the ornaments which, as Isaiah said, "declare their sin." There is no lack of texts which spell out the truth clearly and without equivocation—the great God of Heaven was displeased with those things and used them to symbolize departure from His will.

Turning to the New Testament, the picture comes into even sharper focus. John, in the book of Revelation, describes the scarlet woman of sin (symbolizing the false church) as "decked with gold and precious stones and pearls, having a golden cup in her hand full of abominations and filthiness of her fornication." Revelation 17:4.

In contrast the true church is depicted in Revelation 12:1 as a beautiful woman clothed with the glory of the sun. This woman is called the bride of Christ in Revelation 21:9. Notice that no ornaments are worn by the bride of Christ. These types of the true and the false religious systems also point up the estimate God places upon the use of artificial adornment.

Two final texts from the writings of Peter and Paul will reveal the firm, consistent views of the early church concerning this practice. Both of these stalwarts occupied positions of influence among the disciples, and their Spirit-filled letters represent the unchallenged view of the apostolic church. Paul wrote, "In like manner also, that women adorn themselves in modest apparel, with shamefacedness and sobriety; not with broided hair, or gold, or pearls, or costly array; But (which becometh women professing godliness) with good works." 1 Timothy 2:9, 10.

Peter wrote in much the same manner, except that he especially addressed Christian women who had unbelieving husbands. "Likewise, ye wives, be in subjection to your own husbands; that, if any obey not the word, they also may without the word be won by the conversation of the wives; While they behold your chaste conversation coupled with fear. Whose adorning let it not be that outward adorning of plaiting the hair, and of wearing of gold or of putting on of apparel; But let it be the hidden man of the heart, in that which is not corruptible, even the ornament of a meek and quiet spirit, which is in the sight of God of great price." 1 Peter 3:1-4.

These words of Peter contain counsel for every Christian wife in the church today, and they deal with one of the most perplexing problems that faces Christian women whose husbands are not with them in the faith. How far should the believing wife go in trying to please her unregenerate husband? To what degree should she compromise the truth of God in little things to keep things smooth at home and possibly to help win her husband? Peter's advice is simple and clear-cut. Don't compromise truth and principle at all. Even if the wife is not permitted to speak about her faith she can win her husband by her "chaste conversation." Other translations use the more proper term "conduct" instead of "conversation."

But notice how the conduct of the Christian wife will manifest itself. Peter asserts that she will win her husband much more readily by laying aside the outward adornment. Surely the Spirit of God anticipated the dilemma of the wife who feels that she needs to wear a wedding ring to please her husband, even though she knows it does not please the Lord. This text makes it exceedingly clear that God should come first, and that such a decision also will do more to win the husband than any other course. Hundreds of evangelists and pastors could bear witness that this is true. The women who eventually lead their husbands into the faith are the ones who hold firmly to the standard of God's Word. The ones who do not win their companions are those who will let down the standard in little things to be more compatible with their unbelieving husbands.

This may seem contradictory, but the practical results are demonstrable. As long as the wife is not living up to all the points of her own belief, the husband figures that it must not be very important. He cannot get excited about doing something which does not even claim the full compliance of his sweet, Christian wife. But if she does take a firm stand to please the Lord above all others, even in the face of his own displeasure, the husband is deeply impressed that this "religion bit" must be important. He probably will say nothing about his true feelings. He may, in fact, affect great indignation, but his respect and admiration will be secretly stirred by the firm, conscientious stand of his wife.

We must anticipate right here the argument that is advanced by the wives who are not inclined to part with their wedding rings. They say, "I don't want to give up my ring because it shows that I am married. I'm proud of my husband. I want everyone to know that I'm married. I think marriage is a most sacred and important thing." No one can find fault with these sincere sentiments. Every wife should love her husband, and be proud of him. Marriage is important, and she should want everyone to know that she is married. But let's ask this question: Is there anything in a person's life which is more important than marriage? Yes, there is just one thing which is more important than being married to a husband or wife, and that is to be married to Christ. The claims of Christ's love are the only claims which should ever take priority over the love of husband and wife. In the light of all the overwhelming Bible evidence, we have discovered that ornaments are displeasing to the Lord, our Lover. It is true that the wedding ring will tell everyone that the wife is married to her husband, but it will also tell something else. It will tell that she has chosen to please her husband rather than the Lord Jesus. It will reveal that she is placing someone else's will above the Bible-revealed will of God. As such, it bears a wrong testimony to the world.

Some may object that such a conclusion is too strong. Some are bound to say, "You are judging and testing my Christianity by a little thing like a ring or an ornament." No, this is not the case. It is love for God which is being tested, and the Bible clearly points out the criteria for the test. That test not only involves keeping the plainly revealed commandments of God, but also includes laying aside everything else that we discover does not please Him. Here is the evidence: "And whatsoever we ask, we receive of him, because we keep his commandments, and do those things that are pleasing in his sight." 1 John 3:22.

Please do not overlook the two things which true Christians will always be doing. They obey the direct, overt requirements that God lays down in His law, but they also go further by searching out everything that would please Him. In other words, they will obey the injunction to "always be trying to find out what best pleases the Lord." Ephesians 5:10 (20th Century Translation). Jesus exemplified and dramatized this divine principle in His own life and teachings. He said, "The Father hath not left me alone; for I do always those things that please him." John 8:29. The arbitrary commandments are obvious even to a carnal man, but the little things that please God are revealed only to the loving heart of the Christian who searches the Word for indications of His will. It is a solemn fact that those who will be saved at the coming of Jesus are symbolized by Enoch, who "was translated that he should not see death…for before his translation he had this testimony, that he pleased God." Hebrews 11:5. Paul describes the glorious coming of Christ in 1 Thessalonians 4:16. In the same text he portrays the resurrection of the righteous dead, and the catching up of the righteous living. But, speaking of those saints who should be ready for translation, Paul said, I "exhort you by the Lord Jesus…how ye ought to walk and to please God." 1 Thessalonians 4:1. One of the marks of those who are redeemed out of the earth is their willingness to please the Lord in everything.

Listen, if you know a certain thing is pleasing to the Lord, and yet you refuse to do it, what are you really doing? You are pleasing someone else above the Lord. You may say, "But it's such a small, small thing." Of course it is a small thing, but love is actually tested and proved by the little things we do for one another. Ask any housewife if it isn't so. Her husband may give her a washing machine on her birthday and she would appreciate it. But if he brings home flowers in the middle of the week and says, "Honey, let me dry the dishes for you," any wife will tell you that it means more than the washing machine. Why? Because it reveals more of his true feeling to do the little things than to do big things that are more or less expected. God is pleased when we keep His Ten Commandments, but we really show our love more by going beyond the commandments, to please Him in the little things which are revealed in the Bible.

Right and wrong never have been, and never should be, measured by the amount. It is the quality of sin, not the quantity, which presents the larger problem to the Christian. The Bible reveals the fact that colorful cosmetics, rings, etc. are displeasing to the Lord. The Word of God does not reveal that a certain quantity of colorful cosmetics is wrong, or that a certain type or number of rings is displeasing to Him. Even the smallest deliberate violation of the revealed will of God is serious. It indicates an inward rebellion against placing God first. The devil's favorite argument today is, "A little bit is all right." This was Lot's foolish argument when he was ordered by the angels to flee into the mountains. He begged for permission to go into another city close by Sodom and Gomorrah. His argument was, "Is it not a little one?" Genesis 19:20. Can you understand why he wanted to go into another city after losing everything he had in Sodom? Yet the same rationalization is used by many Christians today. They debate and quibble over the size of their rings, or the amount of the immodesty.

Satan is delighted to hear people trying to decide just how much they should violate the will of God. Never forget this: it is not the degree of the deviation from the Bible standard which is so important, but it is the fact that there is a deviation which constitutes the real problem. The size of the step is not the thing of greatest importance but rather the direction in which the step leads.

Sometimes ministers are accused of making a big issue out of the wedding ring, because they wait for the candidate to remove it before being baptized. Actually, experience has proved that the ring is not the problem at all. The ring is merely the symptom of a much more serious problem—the lack of full surrender. When the heart is yielded, and God is made first in the life, no convert will allow a little ring to stand in the way of uniting with the body of Christ by baptism. When love of Christ is stronger than love of self or husband or wife, then nothing will stand in the way, least of all a small metal ring.

Now we shall give consideration to another aspect of biblical evidence on this subject which some consider to be the most persuasive of all. It answers the objection raised by the few who are still unconvinced that jewelry is displeasing to God. In the most explicit manner it demolishes the last stronghold of defense for even the wedding ring.

Before moving into Paul's eloquent discourse on this point, let us establish a fact which is well known to all who are engaged in full-time soul winning. Those who persist in wearing their ornaments, after becoming members of the church, have been responsible for placing a stumbling block in the path of interested souls. Almost any evangelist or pastor could break your heart with stories of men and women who were turned back almost at the baptistry by the inconsistency of a few church members. After being taught the full Bible truth about Christian standards, these candidates are shocked to see church members, and sometimes church officers, wearing rings or other adornment. Many drop back in disappointment and refuse to join the church.

Someone is bound to object, "Well, they should not be looking at people so much. They ought to accept the truth because it is the truth." This is very good and true, but just remember that we are dealing with souls who are searching for loopholes around the unpopular message of the Bible. It is our business to close every loophole patiently and meet every argument so that they finally surrender in full obedience. The fact is that these people have a right to expect the church to be practicing what it preaches. A few inconsistent members can counteract months of prayerful study and preparation of candidates on the part of the pastor. It isn't right that anyone should be a stumbling block to another individual.

Paul penned the most solemn warning to those who would discourage a single soul in Christian growth. "Let us not therefore judge one another any more: but judge this rather, that no man put a stumbling block or an occasion to fall in his brother's way." Romans 14:13. Jesus spoke out on the very same topic except that He described the enormity of causing a child to stumble. Perhaps His words will have more meaning for us if we read them with children's Sabbath School teachers in mind. "Whoso shall offend one of these little ones which believe in me, it were better for him that a millstone were hanged about his neck, and that he were drowned in the depth of the sea." Matthew 18:6. Serious words indeed! But no more serious than the offense it describes—the misleading of little children who look to teachers as examples. How often have little girls questioned the Bible standards about rings after seeing a ring on the finger of a favorite teacher.

In one particular church, a kindergarten teacher who wore a wedding ring was idolized by a little girl in her department. During the church service the child would often be permitted to sit with the teacher and her husband. Since they had no children of their own, the couple was delighted to have the well-behaved little girl sit with them. She would usually occupy herself with things in the teacher's purse, but, being of an affectionate nature, she would cling to the hand of her teacher much of the time. One Sabbath during the sermon, the woman glanced down at the little girl and noticed she had slipped off the wedding ring and placed it around her small finger. Somewhat perturbed, she recovered the ring and put it back on her own finger.

Week by week, much to her chagrin, she noticed how obsessed the tot seemed to be with the ring. She fondled and caressed the ring, and often tried to remove it unobtrusively, so that she could slip it around her childish fingers. The growing fascination of the little girl for the golden circle became an increasing concern to the older woman. Knowing the Bible teachings about ornaments, her conscience had not been at ease from the time she had started wearing the ring. Now she was unable to enjoy the worship service, as she sought to divert the girl's vain attention from the article of adornment.

At last she could bear it no longer. Under deep conviction that she was placing a stumbling block in the path of the child, she removed the offending ring once and for all. Later, she related the experience to her pastor, and described the feelings of guilt which tormented her for placing temptation before the face of an innocent little girl.

"But I don't see anything wrong with rings. Why should I be a hypocrite and take them off just to impress someone?" This is a question which Paul answers with devastating effect in 1 Corinthians 8:1-13. That entire chapter is concerned with the problem of foods offered to idols. The early church was seriously divided over the issue. The Gentile Christians who had come in from paganism believed that it was wrong to eat such meat. They remembered offering the food in sacrifice to idols. Even though they were now Christians, they still felt it was somehow giving allegiance to the idol to eat the food. On the other hand, the Jewish Christians who had come into the church from Judaism, felt that the food was perfectly good to eat. Since the meat was not "unclean" and since it was sold along with other meats in the marketplace, the Jewish Christians bought it with no question of conscience whatever.

The contention became so severe between the two groups that Paul finally had to deal with it at considerable length in 1 Corinthians 8. Notice his decision in the matter: "As concerning therefore the eating of those things that are offered in sacrifice unto idols, we know that an idol is nothing in the world, and that there is none other God but one....Howbeit there is not in every man that knowledge: for some with conscience of the idol unto this hour eat it as a thing offered unto an idol; and their conscience being weak is defiled....But take heed lest by any means this liberty of your's become a stumblingblock to them that are weak. For if any man see thee which hast knowledge sit at meat in the idol's temple, shall not the conscience of him which is weak be emboldened to eat those things which are offered to idols; And through thy knowledge shall the weak brother perish, for whom Christ died? But when ye sin so against the brethren, and wound their weak conscience, ye sin against Christ." Verses 4-12.

These tremendous verses, with their spiritual focus on love for others, apply with even greater force to those who feel at liberty to wear rings in the church. The application is stronger because the ornaments are condemned by God, whereas the meats offered to idols were not condemned. Still, Paul said it was a sin to eat such food because it was a stumbling block, or hindrance, to someone else. Since the rings have been stumbling blocks in the same way, to other fellow Christians, we cannot escape the conclusion that such an offense is also a "sin against Christ."

This brings us right back to the central theme of this little book—*love*. Whether we are looking at Christian standards from the viewpoint of loving and pleasing God, or loving our neighbor, the result is just the same. The whole idea is to put self last of all. A religion based upon such love will not be satisfied merely to fulfill the letter of the Ten Commandments but will search the Word of God daily for indications of His will. As John reminds us, "We keep his commandments, and do those things that are pleasing in his sight." 1 John 3:22.

May I ask a question concerning what you have read up to this point? Has it raised a doubt about the wearing of ornaments? Does the evidence of all these verses, scattered through the Bible, suggest that the practice is open to question? One couple said, "We are not convinced yet that God would keep us out of Heaven for wearing a piece of jewelry." I asked them, "Even though you don't feel you would be lost by wearing it, do the many texts raise at least some question about the practice meeting the full approval of God?" "Oh, yes," they said, "we cannot say that the issue is not a bit cloudy." My next question was this: "Do you think there is a 10 percent chance that wearing your ring could be displeasing to God?" After thinking a moment, they both agreed that there was at least that much chance that it was questionable. Then I asked them this question: "As you stand on the brink of baptism and the complete surrender of your lives to the Lord Jesus Christ, do you want to run a 10 percent chance of displeasing the Lord who has laid down His life for you?"

Slowly they reached down and began to remove their rings. "No," the husband said, "we don't want to run the smallest chance of displeasing Him. We want to go all the way with Jesus. Since there is a doubt, we'll give Him the benefit of the doubt."

I will not try to pretend that this kind of surrender is easy. Jesus said, "If any man will come after me, let him deny himself, and take up his cross daily and follow me." Luke 9:23. Saying "No" to self is what the Master was talking about. He was saying that everyone will have to battle it out with something that self doesn't want to surrender. The individual who is coming to Christ and learning His ways will have to deny self, or say "No" to something that his whole nature craves to keep. That's what self denial means. Some people fail the test at one point, and others at a different point. I've seen some who could not deny self on the point of money. To obey God might jeopardize their jobs or cut their salaries, and they were not willing to say no to their love of money. Others had to give up friends to go all the way in following Christ, and they were not willing to deny themselves their friends. Appetite has stood in the way of many who were not willing to deny themselves the alcohol, tobacco, or unclean foods as required in the Bible. A few have failed the test on the point of vanity and pride. They have been unwilling to deny themselves the *inordinate pride of dress.*

It is always interesting to see how the truth weeds people out of an evangelistic audience. No one drops out until we present the claims of God which demand a change of life and practice. If we did not preach all the counsel of God, most listeners would gladly respond to the invitation. Struggle takes place when the truth challenges a darling self-indulgence. The tests of the Sabbath, tithe, and diet are all aimed at some element of the self nature. Many fail on each of these points. But strangely enough, the greatest battle seems to ensue when God's will touches the area of personal pride. Vanity is deep and pervasive. Self-love has a thousand faces and exhibits itself in as many subtle ways.

Mark it down, somewhere along the line for every soul the devil will use self to make a last desperate stand against the will of God. Only those who love Christ with all their heart, soul, and mind will be able or willing to make the 100 percent surrender to Him that is required. The happiest people in the world are those who let nothing stand in their way of pleasing God in everything.

It has already been mentioned that Christians who live to please the Lord are the happiest people in the world. Jesus said, "If ye keep my commandments, ye shall abide in my love; even as I have kept my Father's commandments, and abide in his love. These things have I spoken unto you, that my joy might remain in you, and that your joy might be full." John 15:10,11. No wonder, then, that fully committed Christians are so easily recognized. There is a holy radiance and joy shining from within which even transforms the countenance. Although they have laid aside the adornment of the world, they have put on another adornment of the Spirit, which identifies them instantly. Some women feel almost naked after removing their jewelry, but very soon they recognize that God has replaced the artificial with the real. David wrote, "They looked unto him, and were lightened: and their faces were not ashamed." Psalm 34:5.

It is this "new look" of the newborn Christian which has caused the world to marvel. For every evil thing that is given up, the child of God receives a spiritual replacement. As Paul said, "Let us therefore cast off the works of darkness, and let us put on the armour of light." Romans 13:12. And please notice how dramatic this exchange can be when it involves the clothes and adornment of an individual. The bride of Christ receives special attention. Isaiah contrasts the marriage dress of God's people with the dress of the world. "I will greatly rejoice in the Lord, my soul shall be joyful in my God; for he hath clothed me with the garments of salvation, he hath covered me with the robe of righteousness, as a bridegroom decketh himself with ornaments, and as a bride adorneth herself with her jewels." Isaiah 61:10. When we are married to Christ and take His name, we are not to adorn ourselves as worldly brides and bridegrooms. We are joyfully to be clothed with the "garments of salvation" and the "robe of righteousness." This is what lightens the face, and presents the new radiant appearance which amazes the world.

This vital point should be given careful consideration. The face has much to say about a person's character and experience. Our most powerful Christian witness may simply be the witness of our shining countenance. One of the most convincing arguments I've ever heard against the use of colorful cosmetics was based upon this very fact. Frances Parkinson Keyes, the well-known Catholic author, explained why she had never "touched up" her face or hair with artificial adornment: "A quarter century of living should put a great deal into a woman's face besides a few wrinkles and some unwelcome folds around the chin. In that length of time she has become intimately acquainted with pain and pleasure, joy and sorrow, life and death. She has struggled and survived, failed, and succeeded. She has lost and regained faith. And as a result she should be wiser, gentler, more patient and more tolerant than she was when she was younger. Her sense of humor should have mellowed, her outlook should have widened, her sympathies should have deepened. And all this should show. If she tries to erase the imprint of age, she runs the risk of destroying, at the same time, the imprint of experience and character." *Words of Inspiration*, p. 198.

What a tremendous truth is contained in that statement! Christian women have a witness to bear by the expression of their faces. Righteousness, dignity, purity, and calm faith in God—these attributes are often clearly revealed by the countenance alone. Perhaps this is what Jesus meant when He said, "Let your light so shine before men, that they may see your good works, and glorify your Father which is in heaven." Matthew 5:16. The spiritual light and radiance of an unadorned face may attract more attention to the religion of Jesus Christ than a dozen sermons or Bible studies.

We have spent considerable time on the subject of artificial adornment in order to demonstrate how love leads to the Bible, to search out what pleases the Lord. We could just as well have used other examples of Christian standards. The same principles provide the motivation for seeking always to please Him in what we do about dancing, movies, gambling, diet, and dress. It could be shown just as clearly that these high standards of the church are not based upon any committee actions of men, but upon the revealed will of God in His Word.

TELEVISION TRAP

Reference has already been made to the insidious intrusion of the innocent-looking television cabinet into the home. Because there are occasional programs which meet the Bible test of truth, purity, etc., it is easy to succumb to the argument that the set will be used as an educational tool for the family. Solemn resolutions are usually made concerning the high quality of program that will be approved for viewing. But let's be honest and truthful. For how long do those restrictive regulations continue to govern the television set? Policing becomes almost impossible because of the borderline nature of many programs. Uncertainty over where to draw a line, whether a few words of profanity disqualify an hour-long documentary, and other equally perplexing decisions soon become too tedious to tolerate. The door is opened wider and wider, and the discriminative senses accommodate to the increasing flow of below-standard pictures and scenes. It is easy to justify a little more loose language because of the scattered use of expletives by popular network news reporters. Many of the advertising commercials are also laced with innuendos which belittle the Christian moral standards.

It is becoming more difficult to believe that even the most careful selective viewing will not also produce a spiritual desensitivity. Snatches and phrases of gutter talk creep into some of the most highly-touted educational shows. Many argue that we must learn to live with this kind of language because it surrounds us all the time. It is true that we often overhear the vulgarities of the world around us, but should we deliberately expose ourselves to that which we could avoid?

The truth is that most of us face severe struggles in turning away from the enticing scenes of evil that we cannot avoid while walking down the street. There is enough temptation to occupy all of our time and effort without bringing a deliberate source of temptation right into the living room.

What many fail to understand is that there can be sin in a look. If someone had come up behind Mother Eve in the Garden and asked her what she was doing in front of the forbidden tree, she probably would have answered, "I'm just looking." But those looks of Eve led into all the multiplied sorrows and eventual deaths of billions of human beings over six tragic millenniums.

King David awoke from an afternoon nap and, quite by chance, saw his neighbor's beautiful wife taking a bath on her Mediterranean roof-garden. It is more than likely, if someone had asked David what he was doing, he would have answered, "Just looking." But those looks led to adultery and murder, sins which influenced a nation to forget God. The results of his immorality with Bathsheba so marked the family of David that four of his own children were taken from him by tragedy or apostasy. How bitterly he later lamented the scarring consequences of his innocent "looking."

The indelible influence of mental patterns cannot be overemphasized. By beholding we become changed. Thoughts are produced by what a person sees. "For as he thinketh in his heart, so is he." Proverbs 23:7. This brings us to one of the most awesome reasons that television can be detrimental to the Christian life. It is based upon the principle of vicarious or mental participation in the sin.

Jesus declared: "Ye have heard that it was said of them of old time, Thou shalt not commit adultery: But I say unto you, That whosoever looketh on a woman to lust after her hath committed adultery with her already in his heart." Matthew 5:27, 28.

Please take note that the mind is capable of creating such realistic mental pictures that people actually become involved in the imaginary scenes. The participation is so real that Jesus said we are held accountable for what we permit our minds to dwell upon, just as though we were going through the physical act itself. Since the brain is the decision center for the body, every act performed must first be conceived in the mind before it can be translated into action. The brain, through the vast nerve communication system, sends the message for hands, feet or other physical organs to go into action. This, by the way, is the precise point of the strongest temptation. Harboring the mental picture until it transmits the order for the body to act is so presumptuous and so debilitating to the will that few people are able to turn back from obeying the order.

The Christian's only sure protection from sin is to reject the thought or imagination of evil which Satan seeks to impose on the mind. Once the evil deed has been harbored and pondered, even though only as a thought, the incredible intimate relationship of mind and body begins to produce physical reactions. With the speed of electricity the brain sends out the message alerting the entire body to the contemplated action. Now the mind and body unite in bringing pressure for the person to perform the act.

But let us suppose that it is impossible for the person to carry out the physical indulgence prompted by the mind. Perhaps a lustful attitude has been produced in the thoughts, but there is no one with whom to participate in the act of sin. Or if the person is a Christian, he might have such strong inhibitions against the contemplated act that he will resist carrying out the impulses of the mind. In this case the sin exists only in the imagination. But such is the power of thought that, in God's sight, the vicarious mental performance of the sin is counted as serious as the physical indulgence itself.

Now let us apply this principle to the watching of TV. Nowhere do we see a more vivid demonstration of vicarious participation. Even though the viewer may be mature enough to know that the scene is only a fabricated, pretend-situation, yet he becomes as emotionally involved in the picture as if he were actually living out the experience. The heart pounds with fright, the eyes fill with tears, and the viewer is mentally projecting himself into the scene. Whether fighting and shooting his way out of a desperate situation, suffering the trauma of incurable disease, or yielding to the excitement of a provocative bedroom scene, the viewer is caught up in the plot, taking part by proxy in the adventures of the hero or heroine. Jesus said that this kind of participation is just as wrong as the actual physical involvement.

Try to imagine the fantastic strategy of Satan in his use of the television media. It staggers the mind even to think about it. Here is a situation in which the devil inspires one act of simulated sin; for example, an artificial, make-believe portrayal of adultery. But through his manipulation of the emotions, Satan can turn that one acted-out sin into a million real sins of adultery, because a million people will project themselves into the picture. And in their minds it is not make-believe. It is so real that even their bodies react. The emotions of lust and fear so fully obsess the beholder that even though they can't take part physically in the sin, their minds and wills are affected in exactly the same way as if they were taking part. And more serious still, God holds them just as guilty as if they had done it personally.

What a clever, diabolical way to turn people into thieves, murderers, and adulterers! Satan only has to work with the scriptwriters and actors to produce the most appealing, realistic and emotional plots. From that point the natural laws of the mind take over, and the viewers become emotional captives of whatever they allow themselves to look at. One day they may be living out the experience of shoplifting, the next day of murder, and later of fornication or adultery. To the actors on the screen it is preposterous pretense, but to the viewers it is, momentarily at least, an opportunity to do all the exciting things that God and society forbid, without having to face the consequences of doing them. But do we have to face the consequences? Not physically perhaps, but the moral responsibility for those vicarious deeds every person will have to face in the judgment. For those who have not confessed and forsaken those sins, what a terrible account must be rendered for the prostitution of the sacred powers of mind and will.

Surely this principle of sin by substitution explains why the Bible speaks so strongly on the subject of the five senses. Jesus made it clear that no effort should be spared in safeguarding the avenues of the mind. Immediately after His comment about looking on a woman in lust, He said, "And if thy right eye offend thee, pluck it out, and cast it from thee: for it is profitable for thee that one of thy members should perish, and not that thy whole body should be cast into hell." Matthew 5:29.

This text has been often misconstrued. Jesus was not talking about the physical eye. A person could lose one eye and still be evil and perverse. He was talking about the things on which the eye focuses. If the eye is looking at something which is liable to lead the mind to harbor sin, Jesus was saying that the most drastic action should be taken to put those scenes out of view. In other words, "Don't continue to look at something which is spiritually offensive and provocative." Doing so could lead into sin and cause the person to be "cast into hell."

What a dramatic example of the dangers of "just looking" at wrong pictures. Translated into a modern setting Christ was saying that if we have a television set in the home which we cannot control, it is better to cast it out of the house onto the junk pile than to be led into sin by its influence. Better to lead a so-called one-eyed existence without television than to lose our soul by defiling, sinful thoughts created by television.

The command of Christ was to "pluck it out," to turn away from what the eye is looking at. The choice is ours to make. The only way to be pure-minded is to look at, listen to, and speak only the things that are pure. Paul said, "Finally, brethren, whatsoever things are true, whatsoever things are honest, whatsoever things are just, whatsoever things are pure, whatsoever, things are lovely, whatsoever things are of good report; if there be any virtue, and if there be any praise, think on these things." Philippians 4:8. The secret of being pure, honest, and virtuous is to think that way, and the way we think is determined by what we see, hear and speak. David said, "I will set no wicked thing before mine eyes." Psalm 101:3.

To these spiritual factors we could add pages of shocking statistics on the effect of TV violence upon the mind and morals, upon crime incitation, and scholastic achievement. These are well known and oft-repeated. No one will ever know exactly how many blueprints for crime have been carefully detailed in a TV story, and later put into operation by an assortment of muggers, thieves, and rapists.

Society today is in the grip of a growing complacency toward violence and human suffering. Constant television exposure to cruelty and inhumanity has created a climate of amazing indifference to our fellow man. People do not want to get involved. Usually they pass heedlessly by the victim of attack. Public reaction to natural calamities such as earthquakes, floods, or famine is almost ho-hum. The 6:00 p.m. newscast pictures of thousands dying in South America or Turkey make even less impression than last night's late-movie scenes. The animated, bizarre portrayals which have been commercially prepared to impress have far greater response than the actual stories of suffering and death. The fine sensibilities of compassion have been blunted and almost destroyed by the continuous bombardment of the emotions by Hollywood "thrill and horror" specialists.

The impact of death is diminished by the constant overexposure. Even newscast-picture reports of assassination and murder are viewed repeatedly on successive programs. It is almost as though the murdered person springs to life only to be killed and resurrected over and over again. The prolonged screening of Lee Harvey Oswald's murder is an example of such televiolence. The mind finally almost rejects the reality of what is being viewed.

What effect does it finally have upon human conscience and character? No doubt, there is an innate morbid desire to witness violence without guilt. As an innocent bystander the TV watcher is neither the aggressor nor the victim. With nothing to do but watch, and being unable to intervene, he gradually adjusts to a mentality of fascinated inaction. Under constant bombardment, the mind actually blurs to what is fantasy and what is reality. This is why so many are able to stand by and watch brutality and violence in real life without lifting a finger.

A bride recently said, "We are starting out with just the bare necessities of life; a bed, a stove, and a TV set." With 98 percent of American homes owning a set, try your best to visualize the effect of its 6½ hours of operation.

Children spend one third of their waking hours under the artificial, hammering influence of ideas and philosophies which their parents do not originate and often do not even know about. It has been determined that one quarter of the children between 5 and 20 watch over five hours of television *every school day*. This is even more time than they are under the direct instruction of schoolteachers; more time than they play each day, or eat. Only sleeping time tops television as the greatest time consumer.

What type of message is being literally driven into the open minds of these boys and girls? Of all TV programming, 83 percent contains violence, and 98 percent of cartoons depict violent action. In fact, when your children are watching cartoons, they are treated to an average 30 acts of violence every two minutes. Western and detective dramas are not much better, because 97 percent of them contain violence.

But what about the children who are not old enough to be in school? There are nearly twelve million of them between three and five years of age. According to the Nielsen Television Index, these preschoolers sit in front of the tube an average of 54.1 hours each week. Think of the power exerted over the pliable minds and emotions of these near-babies. For 64 percent of their waking hours they absorb the tensions, violence, and nerve-warping inanities of commercial television. Do we wonder why older generations of youth seem to be having difficulty adjusting to real life and people?

Dr. Victor B. Cline of the University of Utah has estimated that between kindergarten and age 14 a child witnesses the violent death of over 13,000 human beings on the TV screen. Since the pre-kindergartners are watching 64 percent of their days, try to imagine how many murders they witness beyond those 13,000. No hard-bitten veteran of daily combat ever came near the horrible mayhem and slaughter of the daily TV fare.

Perhaps the most conclusive study on the subject of TV aggression was documented by Alfred Bandura and Associates, and was published in the *Journal of Abnormal and Social Psychology*. Their conclusions were drawn from actual observation of normal children, measured by reactions of a control group, when exposed to screen violence. Their emphatic conclusion was that filmed aggression heightened aggressive dispositions in children. They definitely do imitate the violent behavior which they view on TV programs.

In 1969 the National Commission on the Causes and Prevention of Violence gave a report on their exhaustive research. Here is the substance of their conclusions: "The preponderance of available research evidence strongly suggests…that violence in television programs can and does have adverse effects upon audiences particularly child audiences."

One of the saddest obvious results of child TV addiction is the tragic breakdown in communication with parents. For those five crucial hours each day there is absolutely no interaction with anyone. Dr. D. M. Azimi, Chairman of the Department of Sociology and Anthropology at the University of Pennsylvania in Indiana, Pennsylvania, believes that children can "hallucinate" on shows filled with violence, sex and aggression. "Interrupt someone watching TV and notice the deep trance he is in. He'll get annoyed with you for breaking into his drug-like reverie, but if you ask what was just said on the program, he won't be able to tell you.

"Parents become TV 'pushers' to their children. Most kids, at a very early age, would like to have a warm, close relationship with their parents. But the parents tell them, 'Go watch TV. I'm busy.'

"Soon the habit takes hold of them and they begin to sit glassy-eyed, in a stupor, 'hooked' by TV. And once they get the habit, it's as hard to take away from them as drugs would be."

If parents do not protect their own children from the incessant emotional assault of television, who will do it? The industry is not concerned about anybody's children. They are intent on one thing—consumption. It takes no expert to see that their primary appeal is to human vanity, lust, and greed. Market psychologists gear their commercials to the wide-eyed innocents who have no defense. Spectacular, hypocritical claims are soon disproved, however, and the phoniness is revealed. The unfortunate aftereffect is a corrosive attitude of cynicism and distrust on the part of the young.

Have you noticed what stereotypes are portrayed on the average TV program? Teachers are generally portrayed as incompetent, vindictive misfits. Happiness comes through as being young and sexy. Marriage is represented as a dull drag, or something to be flaunted by exciting infidelity. Parents are often projected as bumbling, outdated squares with no authority or ability to make sound decisions. The very basics of home and society are subtly undermined by the great majority of TV shows, including some of the most popular ones. It should be no great wonder that our greatest social problem today is how to keep the family from disappearing as the basic unit of society.

LAWFULLY JOINED

Try to picture two kinds of family scenes for comparison purposes. In one home there are three wives, all married to the same man, each with one or more children. The families live together and the husband and father of the three families is always there to give disciplinary authority and security to the overall household.

Now picture another situation. A man has been married to three women in succession. They have all borne him children and have been put away by divorce one after the other. The families are living apart, and the children are growing up under the trauma of financial and emotional insecurity without a father.

Which of these imaginary situations do you perceive to be the worst? The law of the land forbids one and accommodates the other. Perhaps if we could look at all the aspects purely from the social and humanitarian standpoint, we would say that the latter scene is worse than the former. Viewing it from the traditional Judeo-Christian position we would probably condemn the first family as being more clearly in the wrong.

Looking at it solely from the biblical perspective, is there really much basic moral difference between the two situations? According to the Scriptures, marriage is a lifetime commitment. To divorce an innocent companion and marry someone else is even more strongly condemned than the popular polygamy practiced in Old Testament days. Both are frustrating to God's plan and purpose. The children probably suffer more under the divorce procedures than under the polygamy plan, but neither can be defended nor tolerated under the searchlight of revelation. Whether several wives are married at the same time, or in succession, the will of God is violated.

How can we explain the contradiction between Christian practice and Bible principle on this point? More and more church members are acting as if there were no restrictions on the number of marriages they can contract. The moral conscience of entire denominations has shifted and adjusted to the massive incidence of divorce within the church.

Although the majority of Christian bodies have given formal assent to what the Bible teaches about divorce there seems to be very little done in publicizing their position. Church officials and pastors often have to be pressed for a clear-cut statement of the official doctrinal position. The reason for this may hinge upon the embarrassing number who have continued as divorced church leaders with the tacit approval, at least, of the congregation.

Unfortunately, if problems of divorce are not dealt with at the time they arise, it is impossible ever to sort out the issues and take any action later on. Because many such cases involve charges and counter-charges, often unsupported by evidence, pastors are reluctant to be drawn into the explosive morass. Church boards also stay away from the unpleasant task of having to take sides against one of their own who has, perhaps, been a respected past leader in the church. Consequently the issues are left fuzzy. It is easier to give the benefit of the doubt and many guilty spouses are allowed to remain in unconditional fellowship even after remarriage.

Admittedly there are difficult complications which seem to defy human solution. Each individual case is marked by its own bewildering circumstances. There may not be any satisfying answer that will be completely just and equitable for each party involved. But whatever action is taken by the church, it should be in complete harmony with the Bible counsel on divorce, and that counsel is not muddled or ambiguous. Jesus stated in the most positive language that only one condition could justify the act of divorce and remarriage, and that was adultery. "And I say unto you, Whosoever shall put away his wife, except it be for fornication, and shall marry another, committeth adultery: and whoso marrieth her which is put away doth commit adultery." Matthew 19:9.

Please note that Christ charges adultery against a husband or wife who divorces a spouse and marries someone else, *except when that spouse has been unfaithful.* If the companion has been guilty of fornication (porneia, Gr. sexual impurity) the exception would provide for the innocent one to divorce and remarry without guilt.

The unusually severe position of Jesus on this subject of divorce has been the subject of endless debate. Even his own disciples were astonished at the uncompromising nature of His position. They said, "If the case of the man be so with his wife, it is not good to marry." Matthew 19:10. There was no ambiguity in the minds of those disciples about what Jesus meant. They understood that He was forbidding all divorce and remarriage except on the grounds of adultery. Christ's response to their amazement confirms that they had the proper understanding of His statement. Until fairly recently, much to their credit, it can be said that most Protestant and Catholic church bodies have interpreted the words of Jesus very much like those listening disciples did. Unfortunately, with the mushrooming divorce rates, the biblical doctrine has appeared more and more offensive and disagreeable to the growing number of divorcees within the church. Attempts have been made to reinterpret the doctrinal position of some of the churches on the subject, including the Seventh-day Adventist church.

It would be proper, at this point, to consider a sampling of the Spirit of Prophecy counsel which guided the early Seventh-day Adventist church in the strong biblical stand it took on the divorce issue.

"A woman may be legally divorced from her husband by the laws of the land and yet not divorced in the sight of God and according to the higher law. There is only one sin, which is adultery, which can place the husband or wife in a position where they can be free from the marriage vow in the sight of God. Although the laws of the land may grant divorce, yet they are husband and wife still in the Bible light, according to the laws of God." *The Adventist Home*, p. 344.

"Your ideas in regard to the marriage relation have been erroneous. Nothing but the violation of the marriage bed can either break or annul the marriage vow…men are not at liberty to make a standard of law for themselves, to avoid God's law and standard of righteousness…God gave only one cause why a wife should leave her husband or the husband leave his wife, which was adultery. Let this ground be prayerfully considered." *The Adventist Home*, pp. 341, 342.

"There are many unhappy marriages because of so much haste. Two unite their interest at the marriage altar, by most solemn vows before God, without previously weighing the matter, and devoting time to sober reflection and earnest prayer. Many move from impulse. They have no thorough acquaintance with the dispositions of each other. They do not realize that the happiness of their whole life is at stake. If they move wrong in this matter, and their marriage life proves unhappy, it cannot be taken back. If they find they are not calculated to make each other happy, they must endure it the best they can." *Spiritual Gifts*, Vol. III, p. 120.

In one situation Mrs. White counseled that the moral offender should be permanently excluded from church membership. Details of the moral lapse are not clarified in the letter (later included in Vol. 1 of the *Testimonies*). The recommended action shows that some violators of God's law should trust for salvation outside the church.

"It is impossible for E. to be fellowshipped by the church of God. He has placed himself where he cannot be helped by the church, where he can have no communion with nor voice in the church. He has placed himself there in the face of light and truth. He has stubbornly chosen his own course, and refused to listen to reproof. He has followed the inclinations of his corrupt heart, has violated the holy law of God, and has disgraced the cause of present truth. If he repents ever so heartily, the church must let his case alone. If he goes to heaven it must be alone, without the fellowship of the church. A standing rebuke from God must ever rest upon him, that the standard of morality be not lowered to the very dust." *Testimonies for the Church*, Vol. 1, p. 215.

Based upon such statements from the Spirit of Prophecy and the unequivocal statements of Christ on the subject, the position was taken and held through the years that one who deliberately abandoned an innocent spouse to enter a marriage relationship with another person would be committing adultery. They would be disfellowshipped from the church, and, furthermore, as long as they continued to live in that sinful relationship with someone whom they were biblically forbidden to have, they could not be received back into church membership.

This is in perfect accord with the Bible requirements of repenting and forsaking the sin. "He that covereth his sins shall not prosper: but whoso confesseth and forsaketh them shall have mercy." Proverbs 28:13.

For many years the church operated under this sound spiritual principle with a minimum of controversy and discord. But as divorces became more commonplace in the world, the divisive custom began to make more and more inroads into the remnant church. Following his favorite mode of attack, Satan intruded little by little into the family of God with his pernicious, creeping compromise. Divorces for many unscriptural reasons became more frequent. Later the guilty, remarried spouses were bringing their new companions and applying for readmission into the church.

Often the applicants were talented individuals who had once served as respected leaders and officers in the church. Sympathies were aroused, and deep emotional feelings began to favor the finding of some way to get the disfellowshipped ones back into the church.

Almost anyone can empathize with fine, gifted people who ask for baptism, especially when they appear deeply sincere and committed. It is easy to take the impulsive position that these applicants should be accepted post haste and assigned church responsibilities equal to their ability. But should such a decision be made on the basis of our feelings, or should it be made on the basis of the Word of God? As much as we might want to ignore it or deny it, these people have committed adultery, and are continuing to live in a relationship which the Bible calls sin. If God condemns this state of things, can the church dare to give its approval?

By baptizing and receiving them into the body of Christ, we are assuring the candidates that they are children of God and are received by Him. But how can we comfort people with this assurance if they are still living out of harmony with God's law, and if God really does not approve them? Would it not be offering dangerous consolation which might lull them into a fatal acceptance of a nonexistent security?

Some might object to this course on the basis that forsaking the sin in this instance would involve breaking up another marriage, and two wrongs could never make a right. The answer to that objection is that we should not urge upon them what to do about their relationship. We can and should tell them exactly what the Bible says on the subject. Indeed, these people knew that truth long before they willfully involved themselves in the adulterous marriage. This is what makes their situation so serious. The church should make it very clear that it can give them no comfort and approval beyond what the Bible gives.

No pastor has any right to make an exception to what the Word of God teaches about adultery. The church and its ministers should let this couple know that there is no earthly authority which has a right to go beyond the counsel of God; therefore they do not qualify biblically to enter the body of Christ. This is not saying that they cannot be saved. God has authority to make any exceptions He wants to make on the day of judgment. In His omniscience He understands the motives and secret circumstances, but He has not given His church the right to make exceptions, neither the conditions under which those exceptions could be made. Lines must be drawn where they are drawn in the Bible, and emotional personal sympathies should not be allowed to weaken that decision.

Even if a church or pastor could be found who would accept a couple into church membership, even though they were living in an adulterous relationship, this would not enhance their chances of being saved. God's disapproval of the sin of divorce and adultery must be registered so as to impress the guilty ones of the awful nature of this transgression. Under the convictions of the Holy Spirit they will have to decide what to do about their unlawful marriage. No one should urge them to break up their present marriage. They must decide what should be done for their own salvation. Whatever their decision, the church should then encourage them to be faithful, attend church, and trust in the mercies of God. But to accept them back into the church would be altering God's Word to meet our desires instead of God's conditions.

MUSIC AND MOODS

No study of Christian standards would be complete without considering the influence of music. Multiplied millions of young people all over the world have been brought under the hypnotizing spell of rock-and-roll. Like a common denominator, it has crossed the boundaries of language, culture, and religion to affect more lives than almost any other social force. Even the Christian church has been invaded by so-called "gospel rock" which has become the evangelistic vehicle of church young people in communicating with other youth. But what message is being communicated by the tempo and rhythm of this "now" music? How can we explain the obsessive devotion of so many millions to the same kinds of sounds?

Very few people understand the tremendous power that music exercises over the conscious and the subconscious nature of those who listen to it. It has long been known that martial music, band music, and religious music could produce predictable emotional responses. Moods of listeners have been programmed by certain kinds of music. Vast segments of people have reacted in almost uniform togetherness to the same controlled music. They have been tranquilized into nostalgia or lethargy by soothing melodies, or they have been agitated to actual violence by appropriate "wild" syncopated rhythms.

How does music produce moods? It has now been established scientifically that moods have a biological basis. They are produced by a combination of brain activity, blood circulation, and body chemistry. All these functions are affected in an extraordinary degree by music. Medical research has revealed that nerves of the ear have more extensive connections than any other nerves of the body. In fact, there is hardly a function of the human system which cannot be affected by musical tones. Actual tests have proved that music has a direct influence on pulse rate, blood pressure, the nervous system, digestion, muscles, and glands of the body.

Dr. Schoen makes this remarkable statement in his book, *The Psychology of Music*: "Music is made of the stuff which is in and of itself the most powerful stimulant known among the perceptual processes....Music operates on our emotional faculty with greater intensiveness and rapidity than the product of any other act." p. 39.

The most amazing fact of all is how the physical organs react to music. Since the body only functions when the brain commands it to, we know that music, in some way, has to reach the brain first of all. But what part of the brain perceives the music? One of the most important discoveries ever made in this area has established that music is "heard" in that portion of the brain which receives the stimuli of emotions, sensations, and feelings. In fact, music completely bypasses the brain centers involving reason and intelligence. It does not depend upon the master brain to gain entrance into the body. It enters by way of the thalamus, which is a relay station of all emotions, sensations, and feelings. Schullian and Schoen describe it thus: "Once a stimulus has been able to reach the thalamus, the master brain is *automatically invaded,* and if the stimulus is continued for some time, a closer contact between the master brain and the world of reality can be thus established." *Music and Medicine*, pp. 270, 271. (Emphasis supplied.)

Notice that the music has to be "continued for some time" to produce physical reactions through the conscious, master brain. The repetitive, percussive amplification of sound through the electric instruments of rock-and-roll produces a phenomenon which is better described than understood. *Time* magazine describes it in these words: "The hypnotic beat works a strange kind of magic. Many dancers become oblivious to those around them. They drift away from their partners. Inhibitions flake away, eyes glaze over, until suddenly they are seemingly swimming along in a sea of sound."

The most frightening thing about this whole subject is the irresistible assault of the music upon the emotions and then upon the actions. Since the attack is made through the thalamus, the individual who listens will be affected by the music without even making any conscious decision in the matter. This is why doctors have grasped music as a new way to reach the minds of the retarded and the mentally ill. It has opened the door for music to be used therapeutically to communicate with emotionally disturbed patients. Even autistic children are being remarkably stimulated to respond because they do not have to make any kind of voluntary decision—the music reaches the brain center just by being perceived as sound, through the thalamus. Words may mean nothing to the children, but the sensory level is pried open by the music, providing access to the conscious brain.

Now this fascinating fact about music, though beneficial in reaching the mentally disturbed, has also provided a way for Satan to make a sneak attack upon almost anyone who will listen to the wrong kind of music. Without his even realizing it, the listener's mind will be bent to whatever emotional attitude the devil wants to incorporate into the musical beat. Van deWall sums it up in this manner, "Much of what we call irresistible in music is so because we react on this sensory-motor level of functioning." *Music in Hospitals*, p. 15.

Later in his book Van deWall describes how the nerves transmit the music message to the various parts of the body: "Sound vibrations acting upon and through the nervous system give shocks in rhythmical sequence to the muscles, which cause them to contract and set our arms and hands, legs and feet in motion. On account of their automatic muscular reaction, many people make some movement when hearing music; for them to remain motionless would require conscious muscular restraint." Page 106.

With this summary of the subtle psychological effect of music on the brain and the body, we are better able to understand how the rhythm and beat of modern rock music has created so much moral havoc among the young. The incessant themes of illicit sex, drugs, and rebellion have been dinned into the brain, creating an emotional attitude of acceptance toward these aberrations of conduct.

By operating through the thalamus, Satan bypasses the mental and spiritual barricades of intelligent reason, and enters the citadel of the mind—the great control center of all human decisions and action. There, in the mind, Satan has the equipment to translate sensual musical impressions into physical action. Through the telegraphic network of nerves reaching every part of the body, he can communicate the appropriate commands to act in accordance with the emotional stimuli of the music.

It has been no secret that some of the most popular rock-and-roll musicians are not only tied in with drugs but also with spiritualism. Bob Larson has documented the confession of some such performers that their success has been guaranteed by a covenant with Satan. This means that Satan is controlling the production of the music as well as the manner of its communicating with the listener. No great wonder then, that many rock-and-roll concerts have turned into orgies of obscenity, where both performers and listeners are virtually emotional pawns of satanic control.

Many have defended rhythmic music on the basis that it correlates with the natural body rhythms in producing more coordinated activity and accomplishment. It is certainly true that specially selected music increases the working capacity of the muscles. In his article, *U.S.S.R.: Music and Medicine,* Leonid Melnikov enlarges on this remarkable fact. "At the same time the tempo of the movements of the worker changes with the change of musical tempo. It is as if the music determines a good rapid rhythm of movement. Another series of experiments on students proved that not only the working capacity changes under the influence of music, but also the pulse and blood pressure." *Music Journal* XXVII: 18 (Nov., 1970).

Does this bodily response to specifically programmed musical selections mean that all rhythmic musical tones are beneficial to the body? On the contrary, although man has an inherent affinity for certain rhythms, there are some broken-meter, harmonic disso- nances in the melodic line which are completely out of harmony with natural body rhythms. Such is the typical, insistent tempo of rock-and-roll music. Alice English Monsarrat in an article entitled *Music-Soothing, Sedative or Savage,* wrote, "A broken meter in the treble, played over an insistently regular beat in the left hand with gradually increasing rapidity almost to the point of frenzy... is capable of producing the identical disintegrating and almost hysterical effect on an organism; as if a person would try to rush madly in two directions at the same time. Any psychiatrist knows that it is precisely this two-directional pull of conflicting drives of emotions that is helping to fill our mental hospitals with broken wrecks of humanity."

What Ms. Monsarrat is really saying is that to maintain a sense of well-being and integration, people must not be subjected too much to rhythms not in accord with one's natural body rhythms. If the truth were fully known, a vast proportion of the present teen- age restless rebellion might be traced to this constant exposure to incompatible rhythms.

The strategy of exploiting the sensual appetites is not a new approach for Satan. He has experimented with teen-age emotions for almost 6,000 years and is well acquainted with their vulnerabil- ity. He has been delighted to manipulate the lives of unconverted young people through rock music, but he is even more delighted when he can intrude his mind-bending, hypnotic music into the church. By his age-old program of gradualism, he has managed to break down the fine sense of discrimination and to reproduce the same erotic musical beat in some Seventh-day Adventist churches. What a triumph for the devil when he manages to compromise the high standards of the last-day church! Any mingling of spiritual and carnal brings a reproach upon the people who are chosen to proclaim God's last warning message.

The only correct attitude for those who are called out of Babylon and the world is to close every door to the deceptive musical snares of our great spiritual enemy. There can be no compromise with the degrading music forms which have been Satan's tools of corrupting and destroying. We are reminded of Christ's words, "For that which is highly esteemed among men is abomination in the sight of God." Luke 16:15. In the light of this statement we should be even more guarded against music which has become so intensely popular with the world. Only a deep heart experience of love for Christ will empower our young people to take an unreserved stand against this "highly esteemed" deceptive instrument of Satan.

MEAT OR UNMEAT

For well over a hundred years Seventh-day Adventists have enjoyed the tremendous advantage, healthwise, of having special divine counsel on the subject of nutrition and diet. The beneficial results have been documented by scores of researchers and writers. We have a life span five years longer than non-Adventists in the state of California.

Almost every category of degenerative disease is less prevalent among our people than among the general population. This is in spite of the fact that the majority of our membership only gives lip service to the wealth of inspired information on this subject. I've tried to imagine what a testimony this church could bear if every Adventist was a true health reformer.

One of the strongest and most unique contributions of the Spirit of Prophecy writings has been in the area of diet and disease. Over a period of years, in which almost nothing was being said on the subject of nutrition, Mrs. White insisted that meat eating was a basic cause of disease, including cancer. She wrote: "People are continually eating flesh that is filled with tuberculous and cancerous germs. Tuberculosis, cancer, and other fatal diseases are thus communicated." *The Ministry of Healing*, p. 313.

"If meat eating was ever healthful, it is not safe now. Cancers, tumors, and pulmonary diseases are largely caused by meat eating." *Counsels on Health*, p. 133.

During her own lifetime Mrs. White had scant opportunity to see her inspired positions vindicated. Her contention that cancer was caused by a germ, or virus, was completely contrary to all accepted medical opinion. Since her death in 1915, intensive medical research has confirmed, one after another, the principles she introduced. Men like Dr. Clive McKay, world-renowned nutritionist at Cornell University, affirmed that she was years ahead of her time in understanding the subject of diet. She often described health dangers, such as cholesterol, long before the discovery had been made in the laboratories of science.

One of the most recent developments which gives support to our historic position, comes from the National Cancer Institute. Under the prodding of the Senate nutrition subcommittee the NCI released a statement that promises a complete new direction in their basic research. Here is the way *Science News* of October 13,1979, reported the release:

"The NCI's recommendations are based on increasing research findings that diet can be an influence for or against cancer. For instance, cancers of the esophagus and larynx have been linked with alcohol abuse combined with smoking. A high-fat diet has been linked with cancers of the breast, ovaries, prostate, intestines and rectum. A diet rich in unsaturated fats is even more co-carcinogenic, at least in rats, than is a saturated fat diet. In contrast, Seventh-day Adventists, who eat a low-fat diet, have only 70 percent of the risk of others of developing various kinds of cancers. Dietary fiber has been linked with low levels of colon cancer. Vegetarian diets have been associated with resistance to breast cancer."

How unfortunate it is that many Adventists wait until the worldly researchers announce the scientific evidence before they will believe what has been given by revelation. As a result, our health record is not as impressive as it should be. As the evidence piles up indicating meat as a factor in cancer and disease, more and more non-Adventists are turning to a vegetarian diet.

Incredibly, the large block of meat-eating Seventh-day Adventists seems the hardest to impress. In the face of pages and books of divine warnings, admonitions and pleas, thousands of laymen and ministers continue to eat the flesh of animals.

Is there anything ambiguous about the counsel of God on the matter? None whatsoever. It almost appears that those who fly in the face of the counsel have come to a serious credibility crisis concerning the Spirit of Prophecy. If there is doubt in some theological areas which are probed in the red books, there is absolutely none in dealing with the subject of meat eating. Consider statements like these which are representative of hundreds more:

"The liability to take disease is increased tenfold by meat eating. The intellectual, the moral, and the physical powers are depreciated by the habitual use of flesh meats. Meat eating deranges the system, beclouds the intellect, and blunts the moral sensibilities." *Counsels on Health*, p. 70.

"Not an ounce of flesh meat should enter our stomachs. The eating of flesh is unnatural. We are to return to God's original purpose in the creation of man." *Counsels on Diet and Foods*, p. 380.

"Many who are now only half converted on the question of meat eating will go from God's people, to walk no more with them....Far better give up the name of Christian than make a profession and at the same time indulge appetites which strengthen unholy passions....[God] calls for decided reformation." *Counsels on Health*, pp. 575-579.

"Again and again I have been shown that God is trying to lead us back, step by step, to His original design—that man should subsist upon the natural products of the earth. Among those who are waiting for the coming of the Lord, meat eating will eventually be done away; flesh will cease to form a part of their diet. We should ever keep this end in view, and endeavor to work steadily toward it." Ibid., p. 450.

"Those who are in a position where it is possible to secure a vegetarian diet, but who choose to follow their own preferences in this matter, eating and drinking as they please, will gradually grow careless of the instruction the Lord has given regarding other phases of the present truth and will lose their perception of what is truth." *Testimonies for the Church*, Vol. 9, pp. 156, 157.

"I have the subject presented to me in different aspects. The mortality caused by meat eating is not discerned; if it were, we would hear no more arguments and excuses in favor of the indulgence of the appetite for dead flesh." *Medical Ministry*, p. 278.

One amazing fact about this counsel is the way it is rejected by ministers and leaders in the church. With the time of trouble at hand and the flock starving for spiritual direction, pastors are still feasting on the flesh pots of Egypt and causing the people to err by their own perverted examples. Although meat eating per se has never been designated as a sin by this church, what about preachers who do not respond to specific counsel like the following?

"Let not any of our ministers set an evil example in the eating of flesh meat. Let them and their families live up to the light of health reform." *Counsels on Diet and Foods*, p. 399.

"Can we possibly have confidence in ministers who at tables where flesh is served join with others in eating it?" Ibid., p. 402.

"Will any who are ministers of the gospel, proclaiming the most solemn truth ever given to mortals, set an example in returning to the fleshpots of Egypt? Will those who are supported by the tithe from God's storehouse permit themselves by self-indulgence to poison the life-giving current flowing through their veins? Will they disregard the light and warnings that God has given them?" Ibid., pp. 404, 405.

The position of flesh-eating Seventh-day Adventists becomes more untenable when we consider the massive physical evidence pointing to contaminated, diseased meat sources. It is more than stomach-turning to read recent reports of packing-house inspections which have uncovered the grossest violations of minimum sanitary standards. The Consumers Union tested hundreds of hamburger samples from a cross-section of retail suppliers. The test specifically identified fecal contamination, often indicating a disease-causing organism. The startling result of this research was published in the *Consumer Reports* magazine of August, 1971. The objective conclusion of this test indicated that 73 percent of the samples had a coliform count high enough to cause mild illness. In view of the fact that hamburgers constitute more than half of America's beef consumption, we have to believe that a vast health danger is involved, even if we consider only the external handling of meat. Consumers Union estimated that almost a quarter of the ready-ground samples had begun to putrefy at the retail outlet.

An independent check of 68 poultry processing plants by the Government Accounting Office (GAO) in 1971 found sanitation conditions "unacceptable" in most of them. Products in over half of them were contaminated with fecal matter, digestive tract contents, bile and feathers.

But what about the internal condition of the various meat sources? Millions of diseased carcasses are processed through packing houses, and sold to American consumers. At least 80 diseases are common to animals, which can be transmitted to other animals, and very likely to human beings as well. Even proper meat inspection does not mitigate the disease hazard, because microscopic examinations are not possible in the inspection procedures. Open cancerous sores are often cut out of the carcass and the rest of the animal is sold for food. Obviously, the cancer virus is spread throughout the body of the animal.

In poultry alone 26 diseases have been identified which are common to both man and animal. Virtually all chickens carry leukosis viruses, and chicken farmers run six times more risk of dying from leukemia than do nonfarmers.

Meat is the perfect medium for growing bacteria. Putrefaction begins almost immediately in a slaughtered animal and progresses rapidly. There is no way to prevent the deterioration. When the effects of spoilage become obvious through color, smell and taste, large amounts of chemicals are pumped into the decaying flesh to restore appearances. Picture if you can the combined effects of the animal's own waste materials, trapped in the flesh, plus the chemical additives of the animal's fast-grow food supply, plus the external filth factor of the packing house, plus the various injections of cosmetic preservatives. What do you have? A wholly unfit source of protein.

But what can be said to impress Seventh-day Adventists who have not been impressed by the clear statements of inspiration? Those who are ruled by appetite rather than principle will be no more moved by scientific fact than by divine counsel. In the light of indisputable evidence some still feed on hot dogs that contain a mishmash of animal ears, feet, snouts, udders, brains, bladders, eyes, tongues, and blood.

Finally, what are we going to do about the New Testament law concerning the eating of blood? The inspired leaders of that early church spent long hours in discussing the basic requirements for Gentile membership. Their conclusion is recorded in Acts 15:19, 20, where James speaks for the entire Council: "Wherefore my sentence is…that they abstain from pollutions of idols, and from fornication, and from things strangled, and from blood."

How can anyone abstain from eating blood when he feeds on the marketplace variety of slaughtered animals? The flesh is gorged with blood sometimes artificially injected to give a healthy color to rotting meat. To follow the prescribed biblical laws of draining all blood from the animal would render the flesh almost tasteless. Few are willing to deny their craving for animal blood in order to meet the requirements of the Word of God. Various semantical manipulations have been devised to justify eating the blood, but most carnivorous Christians uncomfortably skim past Acts 15. They assume that the New Testament law must refer to drinking blood, instead of eating it in the animal. But that is not the basis for proscribing blood in the Old Testament. Why should it be different in Acts? It is surely something for Seventh-day Adventists to weigh carefully, especially in the light of additional counsel.

I sincerely hope that no Seventh-day Adventist reading this book will presume to scoff at the position here taken. Some ministers have told me about being ridiculed and shunned by their fellow ministers because they would not eat meat with them. It is serious enough to disobey the counsel of God, but to mock at the divine message and seek to make others disobey must approach open blasphemy. The light we have on the subject is far beyond that which was revealed to the historic church of the past.

To reject that light is to reject the work of the Holy Spirit, who inspired the writings. And though we cannot measure degrees of guilt in those who had no light on this subject, we cannot be guiltless if we flaunt the very message which is sent from God to make us a holy and healthy people. Pastors, church officers, and members should repent before God for ignoring His revealed will. Sin is the deliberate violation of known truth, and this makes Seventh-day Adventists, with their advanced light, more accountable before God. By living and sharing that light we not only reap the physical and spiritual benefits ourselves, but become a savor of life unto others also.

POTLUCKS AND PRINCIPLES

The Seventh-day Adventist church is not just another denomination. It is a movement raised up in response to prophecy to finish the Reformation. But what has happened to its program of "reform" which once touched almost every phase of Christian living? The reform of diet has been a trademark of the remnant church from its earliest beginnings, but that right arm has been slowly deformed through being gradually conformed to fleshly appetite.

In too many cases the great governing principles, based upon cooperation with natural law, have been slowly watered down and washed away. Adventist potlucks have become almost synonymous with over-indulgence. Except for the absence of meat on the groaning boards, the after-sermon fellowships have featured the same unhealthy mountain of sweets and spices which lure the world into gluttony.

The control of appetite is the basic victory which must be gained, through the power of Christ, to redeem the tragic indulgence of our first parents. Our Lord faced the issue squarely in the wilderness. Through prayer and reliance upon the Word, He overcame the tempter on the same point in which the first Adam miserably failed. This is the victory which every child of Adam must claim in order to be saved.

How has the original concept of health reform become so distorted that non-Adventists can only remember that we don't eat meat? What happened to the principles of exercise, right combinations, unrefined foods, little sugar and salt, no eating between meals, whole grains, no drugs, plenty of water, and not eating too much? Hundreds of thousands believe and keep the Sabbath, but are actually digging their graves with their teeth.

Almost imperceptibly a change has taken place among our people over the care of the body. No, we have not forgotten the texts about the temple of God. We still pride ourselves on refraining from pork and seafood, and probably 50 percent of Seventh-day Adventists have given up flesh foods entirely. But this is not the health reform message in its entirety. Nowhere has Satan's argument about little things been more effective. By rationalizing over small transgressions, the appetite has strengthened its hold over the bodies of Seventh-day Adventists. Obesity is just about as prevalent among us as it is in the world.

It would be interesting to conduct a survey that would give a true reading concerning self-denial. How many members of our church really say "No" to their appetites? Would it be found that most of them eat just about the way their appetite dictates, without restraint or restriction? Perhaps you should stop reading this for a moment and answer the questions for yourself. Do you deliberately curb and restrict your desire to eat more than you need? Are you able to pass by the dessert tables with their dangerous assortment of sugary pastries? How often do you yield to the temptation to nibble between meals?

Too many have minimized these matters as being unimportant, but they are a considerable part of the great body of inspired counsel which God has committed to this church. Many books, with hundreds of pages, have dramatized the urgency of obeying the laws of our body just as carefully as the laws of God. Deliberate violation of those basic laws of our health could unfit us for the kingdom of God. Is that too strong a statement? Let's look at it a bit closer.

Why do we consider it a sin to use tobacco and alcohol? Because it is harmful to the body, and can shorten the life. The Bible says God will destroy those who defile their bodies (1 Corinthians 3:16, 17). Question: Can you shorten your life by not getting enough exercise? Indeed, it has been demonstrated by scientific data that thousands have died prematurely of heart attacks that could have been prevented. Cigarette smoking is not the only cause of heart attack and untimely death. Does this mean that refusing to get sufficient exercise might be just as wrong as using tobacco? Undoubtedly it does. Until Seventh-day Adventists stop rationalizing away these clearly revealed principles, we cannot hope to escape the crippling effects of our transgression.

It must be understood that we are dealing with spiritual matters when we talk about extending the gift of life. We tend to smile away such inspired counsel as "Never should a morsel of food pass the lips between meals" (*Counsels on Health*, p. 118), but this is a vital principle of good health. Unless we draw lines to protect the delicate organs of digestion, we shall also continue to experience the same ill health and disorders which plague the rest of the fallen race. Sporadic spurts of obedience are not enough. The power of decision must be called upon. Stern battles with self will undoubtedly take place, but habitual conformity to the divine blueprint will bring its own reward.

In the light of so much counsel on the subject, how can we explain why almost half of our people still feed on the dead bodies of animals? Mrs. White wrote in *Counsels on Diet and Foods*: "Not an ounce of flesh meat should enter our stomachs." Page 380.

"Those who use flesh meat disregard all the warnings that God has given us concerning this question. They have no evidence they are walking in safe paths." Ibid., p. 383.

"Among those who are waiting for the coming of the Lord, meat eating will eventually be done away; flesh will cease to form a part of their diet." Ibid., pp. 380-381.

With the mushrooming growth of pollution and chemical poisoning, we hardly should need such pages of specific instruction to turn us from a meat diet. Some of the most popular meats have been tested and rejected by failing to meet minimum health standards. *Consumer Reports* magazine made an extensive research on hamburgers and gave the results in August, 1971. "A shocking large percentage of the hamburger we purchased was well on the way to putrefaction."

Ralph Nader, whose organization did a prolonged investigation of packing houses, summed up their findings on hamburgers and hot dogs in the *Florida* magazine November 7, 1971:

"All these processed meats constitute an imaginative food innovation; they are often used as a handy and profitable dump that allows the packers to get rid of their scraps, substandard or diseased meat, and their less desirable cuts. All they do is douse all these inferior leftovers with coloring and seasoning agents, and market them to an unsuspecting public. Court evidence has shown that contaminated meat, horse meat, and meat from diseased animals that was originally slated for dog or cat food has often wound up as hamburger or sausage; while lungs, eyeballs, pig blood and chopped hides are mixed into hot dogs and luncheon meats.

"To reduce the stench and foul taste, such meat is frequently impregnated with sulfite, an illegal additive that gives old and decaying meat a healthy pink blush. Since the meat used is often filthy, detergents are frequently used to wash off the dirt and, to stretch profits, so-called binders are added to hold the shreds of meat together—generally cereals, but occasionally sawdust."

Perhaps a word should be said about the Adventist consumption of sugar. Recent medical discoveries have confirmed the Spirit of Prophecy statements as to the detrimental effects of sugar on the human body. But do we, as a people, eat less than the national average of 102 pounds per year? From the scenes around the Sabbath potluck table, it would seem that we don't. The average daily consumption is 32 teaspoons. One piece of apple pie has eight teaspoons and a bottle of root beer ten teaspoons. That's over half the daily average. One banana split contains 25 teaspoons of sugar, believe it or not. No, we probably are clogging our bodies just as effectively, and a lot more deliberately, than most non-Seventh-day Adventists. Excess sugar in sweets of various kinds is commonly associated with obesity, diabetes, hypoglycemia, coronary heart disease and arthritis.

It would seem quite unnecessary to admonish Adventists about the wrong in using caffeinated beverages, but we are living in that age of creeping compromise. Strange as it may seem, this first cousin to nicotine has slowly wormed its way into many Seventh-day Adventist pantries. The old Lot philosophy, "Is it not a little one?" has justified the use of a little more and a little more. Beginning with the 3 percent variety, the taste and the addiction for caffeine has been indulged until the habit is fixed.

What is God's counsel about it? "Tea and coffee drinking is a sin, an injurious indulgence, which, like other evils, injures the soul." *Counsels on Diet and Foods*, p. 425. From this statement one might deduce that decaffeinated coffee is only 3 percent sin, but it may be more than that. The fact is that if all caffeine could be removed, the drink would still be highly detrimental. Quite apart from the caffeine, coffee contains caffeol, a volatile oil which gives the unique taste and aroma. It is the caffeol which does more damage to the stomach than the caffeine. In an interview published in *U.S. News & World Report*, Dr. Joseph F. Montague, a leading authority on intestinal disorders, made this statement about caffeol: "If you take a cup of coffee before you add milk or sugar and let it stand a minute, you will see oil float to the surface and swirl around. These oils are very irritating to the stomach and duodenum, and to my mind are productive of more irritation, more preulcerous conditions than anything else people eat. When a person takes this coffee in the morning, he is pepped up. But in reality he simply tightens the screw that holds the string of nervous tension." *U.S. News & World Report*, February 26, 1968.

The cola drinks are required by law to contain some caffeine but not more than about 50 milligrams per ten-ounce bottle. Coca-Cola derives its flavor from the coca leaf, while other cola drinks are made from the kola nut. Please note that coca leaf is the sole source of cocaine, one of the most potent drugs, whose medicinal use is severely limited and supervised. The company claims that all the cocaine has been removed, but repeated efforts to learn the effectiveness of such a process have been in vain.

Many people do not understand that Dr. Pepper is also a caffeinated beverage, containing slightly more caffeine than the Coca-Cola. Not only have Food and Drug Administration sources confirmed this, but the Dr. Pepper syrup dispensed at the fountains is clearly labeled as containing caffeine. Large numbers of Seventh-day Adventists, some knowingly and others ignorantly, continue to consume the addictive Dr. Pepper, which is possibly more harmful than the worst cola drink.

Surely the time has come to throw off this cloak of compromise and follow consistently the grand pattern of truth that has been committed to this church. Revival and the latter rain are awaiting those who will stand firmly on the side of undivided obedience— an obedience rooted in a deep, spiritual, personal commitment to Jesus Christ.

DESTROYING YOUR WITNESS

Suppose some giant computer could make a faithful record of all our thoughts as well as our words. Would we be pleased to see the results spread out before us? It would probably be a shocking experience to see the concrete evidence of what we consider the most important matters in life. What do we think about the most? What subject is so important to us, so dear to our hearts, that we talk about it more than any other topic? Most of us, as Christians, would like to believe that the computer printout would reveal thoughts and words about Jesus and His glorious truth, above all other subjects.

Surely our spiritual commitment should take priority over every earthly competitor for our time and attention, including family and job. The personal relations with Jesus Christ must be given absolute and unchallenged recognition as the supreme issue in the life of every Christian. Jesus taught that we should love Him more than father or mother, husband or wife, son or daughter. He said also, "Whosoever he be of you that forsaketh not all that he hath, he cannot be my disciple." Luke 14:33. Talk about priorities! Anything that gets in the way of serving Christ should be immediately put out of the way. Anyone who begins to compete with God for the highest place in our affections should be instantly denied that position.

Obviously then, the focus of every Christian should be upon spiritual things. Every aspect of his life should revolve around the one great center of serving God and sharing Him with others. This does not mean that most of our time will be spent in church. It does not imply either that we stay on our knees through much of the day. The fact is that family, profession, and friends will occupy most of the waking hours of every week. But the centrality of Christ in the life does mean that all the related activities of earning a livelihood, relaxing with the family, and associating with friends will be permeated with the sweet Spirit of an ever-present Saviour abiding in the heart.

Not many Christians are able to give sermons or Bible studies, but all can preach powerful sermons by living out the beautiful principles of Bible truth. Regardless of talents, education, or profession, every Seventh-day Adventist should be a soul-winning witness of the obedient life.

We do not have an ordinary message. Our doctrines are thrilling, life-changing principles taken directly from the Bible. We can cite the example of Jesus and the apostles for every one of the standards held by this church. We are the "remnant," or last end piece, of the New Testament Church. This is why we keep the Sabbath just like they did. We eat and drink to the glory of God by abstaining from harmful foods. So did the apostles.

Being filled with love and desiring to run no risk of displeasing the Saviour, we obey the injunctions of the Scriptures against worldly adornment and vain attire. The foot-washing service is peculiar to our worship, but it was given by the example of Jesus Himself. Our distinctive life-style touches every phase of daily conduct. It is all bound up with our religion and our spiritual commitment.

Christ is coming very soon. These final probationary moments are for preparing to meet Him. Others may not believe this, but we know it is true. There is no time to waste on the inanities of TV, dancing, theater, and worldly pleasures. By the power of consistent holy living we must draw others away from the emptiness of materialism. Satan is almost having his way all around this polluted planet. Even popular religion has been infiltrated and manipulated by him.

One stubborn pocket of resistance stands against the evil one, and that is the remnant church. No heavier responsibility ever rested upon any people than upon those who represent the final warning message of truth in this generation. We are a savor of life or death to multitudes who linger in the valley of decision. Every soul will be drawn to join us in obeying this message, or else will receive the mark of the beast by rejecting it.

Everything we do will influence the people we meet to make a decision—a decision for or against the truth. What do our words, actions, dress, and diet say to those whose only sermon will be what they see in us? Many of them will be under conviction, but they will also be looking for a loophole around the unpopular demands of truth.

Whether we like the idea or not, our lives will be under the searchlight of scrutiny. Half-convinced to go ahead in faith to obey the Word of God, many will look to us for encouragement. Some will be wrestling over the Sabbath question. Their family business establishment will have to close on the Sabbath if they decide to be baptized. They need to know that it is all-important to honor the Lord of the Sabbath by keeping His day holy. What will they see in us? Would your Sabbath-keeping right now show them the joy of putting Christ first? Or would they see you eating out in a restaurant for Sabbath dinner, causing them to question as to whether it really is all that important to close their own commercial enterprise on the Sabbath? If they are given the idea that the Sabbath is only a holiday and not a holy day, they will make a quick decision to stay right where they are. If Sabbath-keeping is just like Sunday-keeping, then maybe they can justify keeping their employees on the job that day.

Some judgment-bound souls will be struggling over the problem of giving up unclean foods. Convicted and convinced about the body temple, they look around in the church for strength to make the difficult break. What do they see? I'll tell you what one person saw. I know, because it happened just two weeks ago from this writing, in one of my crusades. A young mother had made her decision for baptism. A few days before the baptism she was invited to the home of a Seventh-day Adventist lady. While there she was offered a cup of coffee. Only a week earlier she had, with severe trauma, made the break with a lifetime habit of drinking coffee. Although she explained this to her new Adventist friend, she was still urged to go ahead and take the coffee. She held her ground, but the next day she faced me with some questions that I had a hard time answering. Unfortunately, that lady did not follow through with baptism, and has not at this writing. Coffee drinking does not appear as a small thing when it causes a soul to make a decision against obeying the truth. Christian standards are tied to the Christian witness, and thousands are destroying their witness by the distorted notion that little things don't matter.

Every lady who enters the remnant church passes through the throes of decision over makeup and jewelry. It is not easy to change the customs of time and tradition, especially when they are rooted in feminine vanity. Fashion is a slavemaster. Sometimes husbands are opposed to everything the new religion is doing to their wives, and when they remove the wedding ring with the other ornaments, it precipitates a real crisis in the family. Convicted by the Word of God these ladies decide to put God first, and to accept the challenge of Peter to win their unbelieving husbands by removing their ornaments (1 Peter 3:1-3). Then they look around the church for support and approval. What do they see? Not only a sprinkling of wedding rings, but flashing brooches, pins, and costume jewelry. Are they encouraged? Yes, they are encouraged to go ahead and wear the wedding ring; and if symbolic rings are acceptable, then the class rings, birthstone rings, engagement rings, and friendship rings are all right too. And perhaps even the sentimental earrings that Grandma passed along as a remembrance.

Are we talking about practical things? Does it really happen? Indeed it does, and many are turned away from the truth because the members are not living what they preach. Some ladies are devotees of style, and find it hard to give up the vanities of the world. They see just enough dyed hair, wigs, and artificial adornment in the church to comfort them in their own worldly pride. Their questions about wearing slacks and pants are also settled quickly as they see them walking into the sanctuary on Sabbath morning and Wednesday night.

The problem is that no one can ever win the victory over an enemy that they secretly admire. Many sisters in the church have a secret love of the world, and have, therefore, never been able to win the battle against sinful pride and worldliness. Until they learn to love Jesus supremely and are willing to deny self, they will continue to be stumbling blocks to others.

What will it take to arouse and revive the church on these crucial issues of Christian living? How can we get the church members excited about the truth, so that it fills their lives? When evangelistic meetings are held every member should be there, eager and enthusiastic about the opportunity to share the truth. Tragically, only a faithful few of the members support the meetings night by night as the message is presented. I've seen fine men make their decision in the crusade and join the church. Later they are invited to the homes of deacons and elders who gave only token support to the evangelistic meetings. But in those homes the new member is invited to spend an afternoon looking at a ball game on TV. There the church leader finally gets excited, but alas, it is over the fanatical excesses of one team trying to beat down and humiliate another team. With shouts and uncontrolled excitement he sits for hours, completely absorbed in an activity that is the very antithesis of everything Jesus stood for and taught. That deacon knows all the batting averages and league records, but he'll sit next Sabbath half asleep in church and will not know a single answer in the Sabbath School class. He will probably give his ingathering goal and will do lip service to the lay activity plans for literature distribution, but his life interest is not God's work. Like Mrs. Lot he is bound to the things of the world, and all his stereotyped, platform-religious functions will not change the sentence of death against him. Until that man becomes more vocal about soul winning than he is about a ball game there can be no hope for his salvation. This is why the great majority in the church today will be shaken out. Little by little, they have allowed the world to nibble away their experience, followed by the loss of Christian standards. Finally, only a dead form remains—a form that will crumble quickly under the stresses of the time of trouble.

After the ball game is over it is not hard to imagine that our new male member might question his Adventist host about the correct procedure for tithing. Being a businessman he has a little misunderstanding about gross income and net pay. Also, what about the offerings beyond the tithe? Can people really afford to give more than ten percent of their income? It has been a tremendous step of faith for this man to make his decision for baptism because of a financial crisis in his business which made it seem insane to start tithing. Now he feels the need of reassurance from a leader in the church who will be able to confirm the promises of the Bible.

It may well be that the deacon will bear a thrilling testimony of God's miracle grace in behalf of those who are faithful stewards. Being an officer in the church he would be one of the 51 percent who are faithful tithers. Incredibly, there is a 49 percent segment of our world membership who are not tithing at all. Perhaps some have no income, but many are literally stealing from God every week by misappropriating His holy tithe. With this fact before us it is easier to understand how that greater proportion of God's people will be shaken out in the testing time.

Perhaps more Adventists will be lost over the issue of money than any other factor. This may explain why Jesus had so much to say about stewardship. In these days of materialistic plenty it would seem logical for Satan to concentrate on this device. There is an innate selfishness within the carnal heart of man which Satan is successfully exploiting today.

Is it not a reasonable and extremely advantageous arrangement for a tenant to cultivate a farm, keeping 90 percent of the harvest, and yielding up 10 percent to the owner of the property? Everything that passes through our hands belongs to God and He is merely allowing us to use it. How good and gracious He is to ask only a tithe which is assigned back by Him to use in preaching the Gospel.

Do the promises of faithful giving mean what they say? Will God rebuke the devourer? And what about giving beyond the tenth? Jesus said, "Give, and it shall be given unto you; good measure, pressed down, and shaken together, and running over." Luke 6:38. In other words, we cannot outgive the Lord. No matter how drastically we stretch our faith and try to give a sacrificial amount, it always comes back to us in some way. The promises of God cannot fail.

Most people suffer from pocketbook protectionitis. Whether they have little or much there is a propensity to grasp it tightly and try to get more and more and more. Jesus indicated that few rich men would make it into heaven. This is not because it is a sin to have money or property. Some wealthy people are dedicated Christians and they will be saved. There are really only two kinds of rich people—those who have made themselves rich and those whom God has made rich. By giving liberally some have claimed the overflowing blessings of the Bible promises. They keep pouring it out and God keeps pouring it back in greater measure.

Some may object and say, "That doesn't make sense. There is only a certain amount of money to deal with, and it can only go so far." The ones who raise such objections are sincerely perplexed because they have not experimented with the promises, and it does seem presumptuous and unreasonable. We can just as well explain how the loaves and fishes fed a multitude as we can comprehend how we get more by giving more. But those who have stepped out in faith to do it know that it happens. They don't try to explain it. It will not work out on paper, but the more they give to the Lord the better off they become financially.

I'll never forget being challenged by a friend years ago to put God to the test. He was giving 25 percent of his income to God and had prospered tremendously. My wife and I decided to take God at His word. We stepped out into an apparent giving plan of great sacrifice, but we have yet to catch up with the sacrifice. Gradually, our giving increased from 25 percent to 30 percent to 35 percent and almost to 40 percent one year, yet we have increased in material blessings as our faith increased. How thankful we have been that someone urged us to test the promises of God. Now we feel so sorry for those who have missed the thrill of seeing God do the impossible by multiplying the loaves.

In a thousand cities, towns, and villages around the world the work of God languishes for lack of funds. This should be the smallest problem facing the remnant church today, because God has given the means to His people for finishing the work. What an account we must settle some day if we hold that money and property until it is worthless. Now it can be used to prepare souls for the Kingdom. Jesus urged His people to lay up treasure in heaven by using the money, not storing it away to rust and mildew. Millions of dollars have been willed to godless children by Adventist parents who should have known that it would be used to advance the devil's cause instead of the truth. That money could have hastened the coming of Jesus and the restoration of all things.

Jesus spoke of the "deceitfulness of riches," in Matthew 13:22. Will that deceit involve Seventh-day Adventists who plan some day to place their property upon the altar for God? Many right now are watching the last opportunity pass by in which their accumulated wealth could be utilized for the cause. In the face of a miserable giving record they live in luxurious ease. How true Christ's words, "For where your treasure is, there will your heart be also." Matthew 6:21. When the money has been invested in God's work, the giver's heart is bound up with the work as well. These are the exceptional ones who will not be deceived by riches, but will have treasure in heaven.

LEGALISM OR LOVE

The focus of this book has been on little things, and how Satan nibbles away at the high spiritual standards of God's people. We have analyzed the psychological pattern of gradual compromise by which the power and effect of the truth has been diluted. Some would suggest that we are majoring in minors and that such concern is over trivia which only detracts from the important issues. They question that the God who created the universe could be even slightly interested in the details of individual human conduct. They would label such concern as legalism. But is it legalism or love?

Even if each tiny lowering of the standard did not lead to large departures from the truth, there is another important reason for being particular about the smallest deviation from God's will. Christianity is not based upon prohibitions and rules—not even such highly esteemed rules as the handwritten Ten Commandments. In fact, Christianity rests upon a love relationship with a person, Jesus Christ. The foundational basics of the true Christian life are summed up in the two great commandments Christ gave in Matthew 22:37-40, "Thou shalt love the Lord thy God with all thy heart, and with all thy soul, and with all thy mind. This is the first and great commandment. And the second is like unto it, Thou shalt love thy neighbour as thyself. On these two commandments hang all the law and the prophets."

All the writers of the Bible make it very clear that this is really what Christianity is all about. The theme of love is woven throughout both Old and New Testaments, and the *effect* of that love is the *works of obedience*. Jesus said, "If ye love me, keep my commandments." John 14:15. John the beloved wrote, "For this is the love of God, that we keep his commandments: and his commandments are not grievous." 1 John 5:3

Even human love finds no strain in doing things to please the one and only object of affection. Brides and grooms do not count it grievous duty to make each other happy, and they do not fulfill their vows because state laws require it on pain of fine or imprisonment. In fact, they do much more for each other than the law requires just because they do love deeply. Any little thing which is possible to do for the happiness of the other becomes a joy to perform.

It is in the area of small attentions that the test of true love is revealed. Any wife will confirm that this is so. Even a few fading flowers can move a wife to emotional tears, if she knows hubby went out of his way to pick them for her personally. In fact, the most expensive gift would be less impressive than that spontaneous plucking of a few lowly wild daisies. Why? The answer is obvious. It constitutes a thousandfold greater test of love because the husband would only choose to do it for one reason—to make his wife happy.

Please notice that this should be true in our love relation with Christ also. John says: "And whatsoever we ask, we receive of him, because we keep his commandments, and do those things that are pleasing in his sight." 1 John 3:22. The Christian will not merely obey the overt requirements of the Ten Commandments, but will seek to do everything which pleases the Lord. This involves searching the Scriptures for indications of His will, and running no risk whatsoever of displeasing Him. Genuine love will always be giving the advantage rather than taking it.

If God is at all interested in the manifestation of love in His children, then He must be watching with great interest to see how they respond to every small revelation of His will. It may very well be that the greatest test of true devotion to God is the degree of willing conformity to the sprinkled hints throughout the Bible of little things that please Him. And instead of being counted as legalism, those acts may be weighed in the judgment as the highest form of selfless love.

May God help us to search the Scriptures daily to discover how to know His will in our eating, drinking, dressing, talking, and looking. Then may we have the love to apply His desires happily to our daily Christian way of life.

Whatever you think, never think what you feel
You would blush, in the presence of God, to reveal;
Whatever you speak, in a whisper or clear,
Say nothing you would not like Jesus to hear.

Whatever you read though the page may allure,
Read nothing of which you are perfectly sure
Consternation at once would be seen in your look
If God should say solemnly, "Show me that book."

Whatever you write, though in haste or in heed,
Write nothing you would not like Jesus to read;
Whatever you sing, in the midst of your glees
Sing nothing His listening ear would displease.

Whenever you go, never go where you fear
Lest the great God should ask you, "How camest thou here?"
Turn away from each pleasure you'd shrink from pursuing
If God should look down and say, "What are you doing?"

Whatever you wear, can you be very sure
That the feelings it quickens are blameless and pure?
Would your face be unblushing and conscience be clear
Should your wardrobe be opened and Jesus appear?

When you think, when you speak, when you read, when you write,
When you sing, when you walk, when you seek for delight,
To be kept from all wrong when at home or abroad,
Live always as under the eyes of the Lord.

Index

Abominations(s), 39, 40, 44, 42, 41

Addiction, 103, 77

Adornment(s), 63, 64, 52, 58, 64, 68, 56, 57, 59, 68, 68, 68

Adulterous, 85

Adultery, 25, 71, 81, 82, 83, 48, 72, 84, sin of, 73

Alcohol abuse, 93

American costume, 42, 43

Ancient Israel, 26

Apostasy, 53, 58, 72 54,12

Apostates, 12

Apparel, 31, 58

Appetite(s), 100, 95, 98, 97, 90

Arthritis, 103

Artificial baubles, 55

Atheists, 31

Authority, 19

Baalpeor, 27

Babylon, 91

Baptism, 66

Baptizing, 84

Bathing, 34, 35, 36

Bathing suit(s), 30, 31, 32, 33

Beach (s), 33, 34, 31

Beat, 91

Bible instruction, 36

Bible studies, 33

Bible (test), 70

Biblical doctrine, 81

Biblical laws, 97

Blasphemy, 98

Blood, 97

Blood pressure, 90

Body rhythms, 89

Bracelets, 55

Brain center(s), 87

Businessmen, 41

Caffeinated Beverage, 104

Caffeine, 103, 104

Caffeol, 103

Camouflages, 8

Camp meeting, 32, 34

Cancer virus, 96

Cancer(s), 93, 94, 96

Cancerous germs, 93

Cancerous sores, 96

Carnal man, 25

Carnal nature, 23, 25

Cartoons, 76

Character, 69

Chemical additives, 97

Chemicals, 96

Chicken farmers, 96

Children, 77, 78, 80, 88

Children of Israel, 53

Cholesterol, 93

Christ's righteousness, 12

Christian, 36, 48, 24, 49, 71, 98, 23, 25,

Christian(s), 36, 49, 56, 26, 47, 51, 94, 13, 115, 114, 15, 97, 67, 17 ,60

Christianity, 113, 51, 114,

Church (the), 48, 82, 63, 14, 85, 98, 48, 36, 80, 97, 98, 45, 12

Church members, 14,50

Church membership, 85

Church officers, 63

Cigarette smoking, 110

Clothes (masculine), 44, 68

Clothing, 25, 42

Cocaine, 104,103

Coffee, 103, 108

Cola drinks, 103

Coliform, 9

Commandment(s), 114, 61, 49, 66, 67, 11, 60

Commandments of God Commitment(s), 47

Compromise, 59, 13, 16, 91, 14, 17, 19, 113, 19, 45, 104,

Conduct, 51, 89, 59, 46, 113, 21, 57

Conformity, 115, 12, 16

Conjugal relationship, 23

Conscience, 76

Conservative class, 13

Consumer Union, 96, 95

Contaminated meat, 102

Conversation, 58, 59

Convictions, 9

Cornell University, 93

Coronary heart disease, 103

Corrupt society, 96

Cosmetics, 16, 68, 50, 52, 54, 58, 62

Counsel, 95, 18,

Counsel of God, 98

Covert attacks, 19

Creeping compromises, 20, 31, 83, 103

Crimes of passion, 29

Crisis, 11, 13

Customs, 19, 52

Dancers, 88

Daughters of Zion, 54, 56

Death traps, 8

Defenses, 27

Dessert tables, 100

Devil possession, 28

Diabetes, 103

Diet, 94, 98, 93

Dietary fiber, 93

Dignity, 69

Disciple, 46

Discipleship, 46

Disease, 92, 94

Divine counsel, 97,

Divine warnings, 94,

Divorce, 79, 80, 81

Divorced (legally), 82

Divorces, 81, 83

Doctrinal, 80, 81

Doctrine(s), 50

Dramas, 76

Dress, 16, 22, 21, 29, 30, 31, 25, 40, 41, 42, 53

Dress standards, 30

Dress styles, 40

Dress(ed), 34, 35

Dress (es), 23
Dressing, 115, 40
Drinking, 115

Earrings, 55, 53, 58
Eating, 115
Emotion(s), 90, 88
Enemies, 13
Enemy, 15
Evil minds, 21
Evil Spirits, 28
Exercise, 32, 100
Experts, 41
Exposure(s), 31, 34
External life, 46

Face(s), 69, 68, 56
Familiarities, 32
Familiarity, 33
Family (ies), 79, 78
Fanatical, 16, 34
Fashion market, 29
Fashion(s), 29, 22, 33, 43, 19
Fatal diseases, 93
Female form, 36
Female nudity, 23
Feminine distinctions, 41
Femininity, 41
Flesh foods, 100
Flesh meat, 94, 100
Fleshly appetite, 27, 98, 23
Fleshly lust, 27
Fleshy, nature, 23
F&D Administration, 104
Fornication, 81, 97
Forums, 38

Gay movement, 38, 39
Gluttony, 98
God's law, 29
Godliness, 12
Gospel rock, 86
Great controversy, 11

Half dress, 24,
Hamburger(s), 96,102
Harlot(s), 57, 31
Health, 100
Health reform, 95, 100, 58, 62, 60
Health reformer, 92, 102
Health standards, 102
Heathen women, 54
Heathenism, 58
High fat diet, 93
Holy Spirit, 29, 85, 98
Homosexuality, 40, 42
Homosexuals, 38, 39, 42
Hoops, 42
Hot dogs, 102, 97
Husband(s), 49, 60, 62, 59, 81,
   82, 114
Hypnotic beat, 88
Hypnotized, 8
Hypoglycemia, 103

Idol(s), 65
Imagination, 72
Immodest, 22, 36
Immodest Clothing, 27
Immodesty, 21, 62
Immorality, 71
Imputed righteousness, 21

Influence(s), 71, 8, 9,
Inspired counsel, 100
Instruments (electric), 88
Intestinal disorders, 103
Ishmaelites, 53
Israelites, 53
Issues, 25

Jewelry, 14, 50, 52, 54, 55
Jewels, 58
Jezebel, 54
Judeo-Christian, 79
Judgement(al), 115, 74, 84, 53, 13, 14

Last day events, 48
Latter rain, 104
Law 79,83
Law(s), 49, 82, 50, 114, 60, 100
Leaders, 36, 97, 32
Legalism, 115, 113
Legalistic, 52, 13
Liberals, 21, 45
Liberties, 32
Lifestyle, 10, 14
Limbs, 43
Look-alike boutiques, 38
Love, 66, 48, 114, 115
Low fat diet, 93
Low necks, 31
Lukewarm state, 18
Lower the standards, 18

Make-up, 14, 16
Male nature, 26

Man, 23
Mark of the Beast, 13
Mark of heathen, 53
Marriage, 84, 47, 24, 60, 80, 78, 82, 50, 85,
Marriage (adulterous), 84
Marriage chamber, 24
Married to Christ, 60
Masculine, 44
Masculinity, 41
Massive attack, 13
Master brain, 88
Meat, 100
Meat diet, 102, 100,
Meat eating, 93, 92, 95, 94
Meat eating diet, 100
Meat inspection, 96
Media, 8, 24, 73
Medical research, 87
Members, 30, 31, 41, 98
Membership, 97
Men, 36
Mind, 72, 74, 75, 89
Mingling, 32, 9
Mini clothes, 27
Mini(s) skirt(s), 28, 30, 22, 27, 25, 34, 42,
Ministers, 18, 34, 62, 84, 97, 98
Ministry, 30
Missionary volunteer, 35
Mixed bathing, 34
Mixed swimming, 34, 33
Moab, 27
Modern Israel, 26
Modest, 30, 44
Modest dress, 32
Modesty, 21, 22, 24, 31, 34, 32, 17

Modesty and decency, 28
Moral (responsibility), 74
Moral havoc, 89
Morality, 83
Morals, 46, 75, 8
Movies, 14
Muscular reactions, 89
Music, 87, 88, 86, 89, 90, 91
Musical, 90, 88, 91, 87

Naked, 22, 32, 34
Nakedness, 21, 12
National cancer institute, 93
Natural calamities, 75
Natural laws of the mind, 73
Neckline, 34
Nerves, 88, 89
Nervous system, 89
Nicotine, 103
Non-Adventist, 94
Nose jewels, 55
Nudist colony, 32
Nudity, 24, 22, 25, 26, 28, 27
    Female, 31
Nutrition and Diet, 92

Obedience, 12,114, 100, 104
Obesity, 103, 100
Obey, 52, 52, 60, 61
Obey God, 67
Obeying the truth, 13
Objects, pagan, 52
Ornamentation, 57
Ornament(s), 57, 60, 52, 53, 54,
    57, 63, 65, 68, 64, 58, 55, 66

Packinghouse, 95 102, 96
Pants 42, 43
Pantsuit(s), 43, 42, 40
Parade, 27
Parents, 41, 78, 36
Participation, 73
Pastor(s), 63, 84, 85, 48, 98, 80,
    95, 59,
Paul Harvey, 28
Peculiar, 45
People, 19, 26, 98, 9
People, young, 30, 31, 35, 36,
    50, 90, 91, 86
Persecution, 10, 11
Plain testimony, 17, 18
Plots, emotional, 73
Pollution, 100
Polygamy, 80
Pornography, 24
Potluck(s), 98, 102
Poultry, 96, 26
Prayer, 100, 25
Preachers, 18, 47, 50
Present truth, 83, 95
Pride, 55, 67
Principle(s), 50, 51, 21, 61, 62,
    97, 15, 98, 36, 30, 46, 35, 74
Processed meats, 102
Protein, 97
Proxy, 73
Psychological assault, 15
Pulmonary diseases, 93
Punishment, 48, 51
Putrefaction, 96

Ralph Nadar, 102
Rebellion, 62

Rebuke, 19, 83
Reform, 25, 99
Reformation, 94, 99, 53
Religion, 50, 40, 66, 69, 48, 45
Remarriage, 81, 80
Remarry, 81
Remnant, 10
Remnant church, 98, 42, 41, 27, 24, 17
Restrictions, 48, 50
Revival, 104
Right arm, 98
Righteousness, 69
Righteousness by faith, 21
Rings, 64, 63, 62, 60, 55, 56, 65, 66
Robe of righteousness, 68
Rock & roll, 88, 86, 89
Rock music, 89
Role(s), 40, 41
Rules, 47, 49, 50, 52, 46, 113

Sabbath, 100, 33, 13
Satan, 10, 89
Satan ('s), 12, 14, 11, 26, 8, 91, 44, 72, 73
Satan controlling, 89
Scriptures, 115
SDA, 13, 94
SDA church, 81, 22, 99, 91
Seafood, 100
Seal of God, 13
Self control, 26
Self love, 67
Self-denial, 47
Sequences (rhythmical), 89
SDA Christians, 31
Seventh-day Adventist(s), 100, 97, 104, 103, 95, 98, 92, 13, 17, 10
Sex, 24, 39, 28, 25, 29
Sex (y), illicit, 27
Sexual, 27
Sexual identity, 40, 41
Sexual license, 26
Shaking, 14, 18
Shamelessness, 56
Short dresses, 28
Short skirt, 29, 28
Sin(s), 85, 83, 19, 39, 71, 73, 82, 65, 74, 72, 62, 84, 18, 53
Sinner, 8
Skirts, 17
Slaughtered animals, 97
Socials, 31
Society, 9, 78
Sodom, 16, 17, 39, 62, 55
Sodomy, 39, 40
Spirit of Prophecy, 11, 35, 42, 83, 81, 94, 102, 92
Spiritual, 71, 91, 95, 75
Spiritual benefits, 98
Spiritual danger, 15
Spiritual matters, 100
Standard (Bible), 62, 64
Standard(s), 113, 70, 31, 59, 83, 71, 19, 20, 50, 63, 66, 86, 69, 16, 91, 14, 33, 46, 51
Stiff-necked people, 54
Stimulant, 87
Strait-laced extremist, 10
Strange gods, 52, 53
Stumbling blocks, 65, 63
Styles, 42
Sugar, 100, 102, 103
Swimming, 30, 36, 35, 32

Tea, 103
Teachers, 78
Teenagers, 36, 90
Television, (TV), 8, 14, 70, 74, 78, 24, 16, 75, 77, 78, 76, 73
Television-index Nielsen, 76
Temptation(s), 72, 64, 29, 71, 25, 26
Test, 60, 67
Testimony, 18
Thalamus, 89, 88, 87
The Christian(s), 72
The Church, 80, 84, 55, 18, 34, 36, 83, 12
The truth, 18, 47, 67, 113, 29, 48
The world, 9, 91, 14, 11, 19, 17, 10, 12, 13, 45,
Third Angel's Message, 12
True devotion, 15
Truth(s), 12, 63, 95, 10
Tuberculosis, 93
Tumors, 93

Undress, 32
Unholy passions, 94
Unisex, 38, 44, 22, 42, 41

Values, 8
Vanity, 56, 67
Vegetarian diet(s), 95, 93
Violence, 76, 77
Vital principle (s), 100
Vulgarities, 71

Warnings, 63,95
Wedding ring(s), 60, 52, 64, 57, 59, 56
Wife (wives), 114, 62, 81, 82, 59, 60, 58, 80
Woman(s), 57, 55, 40, 24, 58, 23, 39,41
Womanhood, 24
Women, (Adventist), 42, 59, 69, 79, 23, 29, 58, 27, 54, 33
Women's Lib movement, 40
Word of God, 97, 84
Works, 9
Worldliness, 14
World lings, 10
Worldly, 27, 12, 13, 11, 19,14

Spirit of Prophecy Index

Chapter One — Our Enemy - the World

standard, Seventh-day Adventists, straight-laced extremists, *Fundamentals of Christian Education,* p. 289 (p.10)

solemn time, conform to the world, spiritually dead, *Testimonies*, Vol. 1, pp. 608-609 (p. 11)

base metal, *Testimonies*, Vol. 5, p. 136 (p. 11)

test, false sabbath, Commandments of God, worldly customs, threatened imprisonment, true godliness, Christ's righteousness, *Prophets and Kings*, p. 188 (pp. 11-12)

storm approaches, third angel's message, uniting with the world, men of talent and pleasing address, bitter enemies, Sabbath keepers, agents for Satan, *The Great Controversy*, p. 608 (p. 12)

work which the church has failed to do, peace and prosperity, worldly conformity, fiercest opposition, conservative class, apostates, excite indignation, *Testimonies* Vol. 1, p. 278 (pp. 12-13)

uniting with the world, Mark of the Beast, obeying the truth, Seal of God, *Testimonies*, Vol. 5, p. 216 (p. 13)

Satan will insinuate himself, specious devices of Satan, *Selected Messages*, Book 2, p. 21 (p. 15)

the work of the enemy, secret undermining, *Patriarchs and Prophets*, p. 178 (p.15)

the power of example, *Testimonies* Vol. 1, p. 278 (p. 17)

rise up against the plain testimonies, more dangerous condition, experimental religion, the shaking, peculiarity of our faith, false shepherds, *Spiritual Gifts*, Vol. II, pp. 284-285 (pp. 17-18) shunning of the living testimony, stirring testimony, straight testimony, sins exist in the church, opposition has risen in the church to plain testimony, plain testimony, lukewarm state, *Spiritual Gifts*, Vol. ll, pp. 283-284 (p.18)

too little courage to reprove wrong, held accountable for the evil that may result, *Patriarchs and Prophets*, p. 578 (p.19)

distance widening between Christ and His people, *Spiritual Gifts*, Vol. IV, p. 68 (p. 19)

God's peculiar people, not yield one inch to customs and fashions, no compromise with its corrupt and idolatrous practices, *Testimonies*, Vol. 5, p. 78 (p. 19)

Chapter Two — Is Nudity Modest?

fashion is deteriorating the intellect, obedience to fashion is pervading our Seventh-day Adventist churches, *Testimonies* Vol. 4, p. 647 (p. 22)

our example and influence must be a power, we must abstain from any practice, *Testimonies*, Vol. 5, p. 360 (pp.25-26)

grace of God, spiritual eyesight, evil good and good evil, avenues of the soul, persevering effort, sore discipline, stem conflict, *Testimonies* Vol. 3, p. 324 (p. 26)

Chapter Five — Unisex

not wear that which pertaineth to a man, God pronounces it an abomination, *Testimonies*, Vol, 1, p. 457 (pp. 41-42)

vest, pants and a dress resembling a coat, *Testimonies*, Vol. 1, p. 465 (p. 42)

this dress I have opposed, *Testimonies*, Vol. 1, p. 465 (p. 43)

dress of the second class, prejudice good people, American Costume,
   Present Truth and Review and Herald Articles, Vol. 1, p. 73 (p. 43)

I saw God's order had been reversed,
   Testimonies, Vol. 1, p. 457 (p. 43)

Chapter Eight — Lawfully Joined

legally divorced by laws of land, adultery, marriage vow, divorce,
   laws of God, *The Adventist Home*, p. 344 (p. 82)

marriage relation, violation of marriage bed, standard of righteousness, adultery, *The Adventist Home*, pp. 341-342 (p. 82)

unhappy marriages, solemn vows, sober reflection and earnest
   prayer, *Spiritual Gifts*, Vol. Ill, p. 120 (p. 82)

light and truth, refuse reproof, inclinations of corrupt heart, violated
   the holy law of God, standing rebuke from God,
   Testimonies, Vol. 1, p. 215 (pp. 82-83)

Chapter Ten — Meat or Unmeat

eating flesh, tuberculous and cancerous germs, tuberculosis, cancer,
   fatal diseases, *The Ministry of Healing*, p. 313 (p. 93)

meat eating, cancers, tumors, pulmonary diseases, meat eating,
   Counsels on Health, p. 133 (p. 93)

disease, meat eating, physical powers, flesh meats, deranges the
   system, clouds the intellect, blunts moral sensibilities,
   Counsels on Health, p. 70 (p. 94)

not an ounce of flesh meat, God's original purpose,
   Counsels on Diet and Foods, p. 380 (p. 94)

half-converted, meat eating, God's people, indulge appetites, unholy passions, decided reformation, *Counsels on Health*, pp. 575-579 (p. 94)

His original design, natural products of the earth, meat eating, *Counsels on Health*, p. 450 (p. 94)

vegetarian diet, follow their own preferences, careless of the instruction, present truth, *Testimonies*, Vol. 9, pp. 156-157 (p. 95)

mortality caused by meat eating, indulgence of appetite and dead flesh, *Medical Ministry*, p. 278 (p. 95)

evil example, eating of flesh meat, light on health reform, *Counsels on Diet and Foods*, p. 399 (p. 95)

confidence in ministers, flesh is served, *Counsels on Diet and Foods*, p. 402 (95)

ministers of the Gospel, most solemn truth, fleshpots of Egypt, supported by the tithe, self-indulgence, life-giving current, disregard the light and warnings, *Counsels on Diet and Foods*, p. 404, 405 (p. 95)

Chapter Eleven — Potlucks and Principles

morsel of food, between meals, *Counsels on Health*, p. 118 (p.101)

flesh meat, stomachs, *Counsels on Diet and Foods*, p. 380 (p.101)

flesh meat, warnings, safe paths, Ibid,. p. 383 (p. 101)

coming of the Lord, meat eating diet, Ibid., pp. 380-381 (p. 101)

tea and coffee drinking is a sin, injurious indulgence, evils, injures the soul, *Counsels on Diet and Foods*, p. 425 (p. 103)

NOTES

NOTES

NOTES

NOTES

Books Offered By
Homeward Publishing

Creeping Compromise, by Joe Crews $11.95

Reaping the Whirlwind, by Joe Crews $10.95

Thy Nakedness, Lord, What Shall I Wear?
by Gwen & Rick Shorter $13.95

Jewelry, Adornment, Personal Decoration & More...
 The Spiritualism Connection, by Gwen & Rick Shorter $14.95

Shorter's Health Manual for Vegetarian Cooking
and Nutrition Classes (Total Health Seminar) $29.95

Spiritualistic Deceptions in Health and Healing,
by Edwin A. Noyes, MD, MPH $15.00

Passion of the Ages, by E. G. White (Also in Spanish) $85.00
(per case of 100)

She Kissed the Face of God, E. G. White (Also in Spanish) $75.00
(per case of 100)

In God We Trust (9-11 Memorial Edition, *Steps to Christ*) by E. G. White ... $49.00
(per case of 100)

Add 20% of total for shipping and handling

Payment by Check, Money Order, or All Major Credit Cards

Call for Case Pricing

WWW.HOMEWARDPUBLISHINGMINISTRIES.COM

24- HOUR TOLL-FREE ORDER LINE
1-800-823-0481

Homeward Publishing
P.O. Box 357
Yorba Linda, CA 92885